Organs of Toronto

Organs *of* Toronto

Alan Jackson *&* James Bailey

Photographs
Brian J. Thompson

Illustrations
Willem Hart

ROYAL CANADIAN
COLLEGE OF ORGANISTS
Toronto Centre, 2002

THE ONTARIO TRILLIUM FOUNDATION
LA FONDATION TRILLIUM DE L'ONTARIO

The Royal Canadian College of Organists, Toronto Centre, gratefully acknowledges the financial support of the Ontario Trillium Foundation, an agency of the Ministry of Citizenship, Culture and Recreation. With $100 million in annual funding from the province's charitable gaming initiative, the Foundation provides grants to eligible charitable and not-for-profit organizations in the arts culture, sports, recreation environment and social service sectors.

National Library of Canada Cataloguing in Publication Data

Jackson, Alan, 1926-

Organs of Toronto

Includes bibliographical references.
1. Organ (Musical instrument) – Ontario – Toronto
I. Bailey, James, 1951-
II. Title.
ML563.8. T6J32
2001   786.5'1971354
C2001-911286-6

ISBN: 0-9689713-0-x

Book design & typography: Willem Hart

Printed in Canada by: Printcrafters Inc., Winnipeg, Manitoba

Information
Royal Canadian College of Organists
112 St. Clair Avenue West, Suite 403
Toronto, Ontario
Canada M4V 2Y3
Tel.: 416·929·6400
Fax: 416·929·0415
e-mail: rcco@the-wire·com
Web: www·rcco·ca

Contents

Preface
The first time

I remember the first organ I ever played. I remember it vividly and recall it happily. It was at the old premises of the Royal Conservatory of Music of Toronto at College and University; where the Ontario Hydro building is now, kitty-corner to Queen's Park; and I couldn't have been much more than 12 or 13.

For weeks I had scouted the concert hall, before and after each piano lesson I used to take. The mighty Casavant (three manuals, I believe: Great, Swell and Choir) never had its case shut. I had discovered the on/off button. All I needed was the courage to sit down, press the button, and kick in one of the dozen shiny coupler pistons beside the foot pedals. When that courageous moment came, I wish I could report that it wasn't the "Full organ" piston I went to automatically. I wish it weren't so, but it would be a lie. I kicked it in with gusto then paused for about five prayerful moments, taking in the deepest of breaths, and put my fingers over the keys for a G-major chord. I pressed down.

Oh my God!

That's what I remember. When I figured out that I could ground it all with cannon-fire and deep growlings by merely placing one foot on the bottom G pedal, I had succumbed. Utterly succumbed. Throughout the ensuing years, I have remained in the thrall of organs. Although the Conservatory organ is no more, and although the organ at my own Massey College is not mentioned in this otherwise exemplary and wonderful book, I rejoice at the publication now in your hands, as will anyone who loves organs and knows what an important part they have played, and continue to play, in the life of the city.

John Fraser, Master
Massey College,
University of Toronto

Foreword

When two organists meet the first question is likely to be "What is the organ like at your church?" From there a discussion continues about who built it and when, how many stops, ranks and pipes it has, how many manuals, the type of action, the sound, mechanical trouble, upcoming changes and for some, where it was before it was installed in its specific location. No other musical instrument could evoke such a conversation. Pipe organs are built differently for each situation and to whatever style the art has progressed or regressed. This book is addressed to such matters for the City of Toronto and will hopefully become a lasting segment of the Toronto Organ Festival 2001.

During the week of the Festival, twenty-three instruments were toured, played in concert and competition or used for liturgical service accompaniment. These instruments are all included in this book with details of the stop lists and the accessories available at the time of the event. The specifications were studied in advance by each performer when the composers and music to suit each instrument was chosen. Dame Gillian Weir chose to play Healey Willan's *Introduction, Passacaglia and Fugue* on the organ at St. Paul's Bloor Street, the very organ for which the music was written eighty-two years before. With each passing year, the historical significance of such performances grows along with the popularity of the music.

An additional thirteen organs of special interest are included, some for historical value and some in order to include as many different builders as possible.

A glossary of terms will help the reader to understand the special and ever changing organ terminology. An analysis of stop, ranks, pipes and real stops is included for some of the larger instruments. This provides an approximate comparison of the size of each organ but does not take into account the ratio of large expensive stops to small stops. The 12 largest pipes of a full length 32' open wooden flute would cost over ten times as much to build as a mixture stop with 224 pipes. The stop list, the names and pitches, the borrowings, the type of action and the casework are all needed to evaluate an organ.

To assess the effect of an organ or to understand why one organ sounds well and another poorly requires a description of the placement, acoustics and the architecture of the room. The proportions of a church or hall and the interior finishes and furniture can make a finely built and regulated organ sound dull and inadequate. Under good conditions a poorly voiced, badly designed organ can sound impressive. At least half of the success of the most favoured instruments is owed to the architectural surroundings and the balance to the skill and experience of the organ builder. The builder must work with the restrictions of the space which may be set in stone in more ways than one; an acoustician who believes organ builders always want excessive reverberation; an organist who may have a favourite stop that has to be included even if it displaces a necessary voice; an organ consultant who has ultimate control, and, more often than not, a budget which is too low.

The years of struggle and setback that precede the opening of many new and rebuilt organs are often forgotten but offer tales rarely told. They are certainly not in the text of the monthly reports on new organs as found in organists' magazines consisting of letters of praise from the church council to prove they chose the right builder and letters from the builders with the hype which finds excuses for the way things were done.

There are many hundreds of organs in Toronto, far more than we could include in this small volume. We trust that this book will have helped to draw attention to our heritage and encourage the preservation and protection of the organs of Toronto.

Alan Jackson & James Bailey
Toronto, May 2002

Acknowledgements

Publication of this book would not have been possible without the generous assistance of the Ontario Trillium Foundation, which purchased the first 600 copies for distribution to schools and libraries in Ontario. Application for the grant was negotiated by Thomas Fitches, a member of Toronto Centre and ardent supporter of the project.

The authors wish to thank the Executive Committee of the Royal Canadian College of Organists, Toronto Centre, President Barbara Hallam-Price and the Committee of the Toronto Organ Festival 2001, and the co-leadership of William and Patricia Wright.

Among the many volunteers who assisted were Ashley and Shelley Tidy who edited the first drafts and Kenneth Inkster and Norah Jackson who undertook to read and correct the proofs. Norma Brubacher provided special assistance with development of the book and with distribution. Isabel Jackson gave encouragement and sound advice throughout the years of development of the book then proved it was all worth while by selling ten percent of the total product in the five days of the Festival.

We are most grateful to the many churches, their organists and other staff who so generously opened doors and files and helped us in our search for authentic information. Other contributors of information and assistance included Casavant Historian Simon Couture who searched for files and photos. Other photos are the work of Michael Perrault and of long time supporter, RCCO Life Member Everett Roseborough.

John Fraser has provided the RCCO with many wonderful speeches and receptions over the years. We are honoured that he has made a space in his busy schedule to add one more favour by writing the Preface for this book.

Our thanks go to the team of Willem Hart Art & Design Inc., Willem Hart, Carroll Guen and Brian Thompson who undertook, with great enthusiasm the design, illustrating, layout and production of the book.

Alan Jackson & James Bailey
Toronto, May 2002

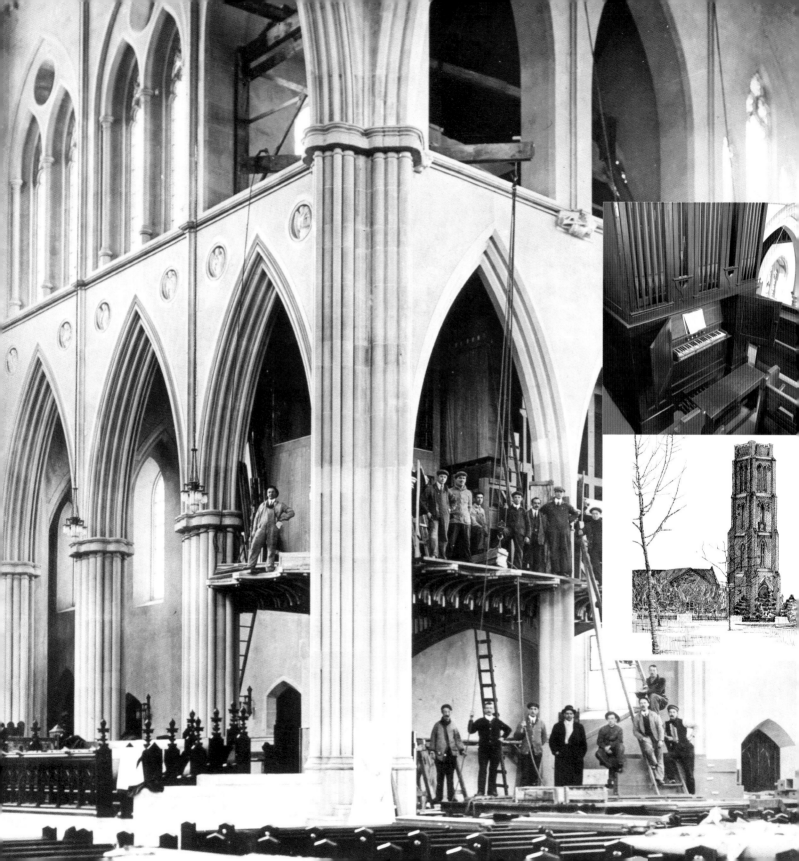

Introduction
Three half centuries

(Opposite) The installation of the Casavant Organ in St. Paul's Anglican Church in 1914. The wooden building frame showing in the far archway is a part of the Tuba Organ expression box. Shirts and ties were worn by most employees in the shop and on the road.

(Opposite, inset) The one-manual Mead organ, originally installed in St. James' Cathedral, restored and playable, in the gallery at St. Clement's Anglican Church.

(Opposite, inset) All that remained of St. George the Martyr after the fire of 1955 was the graceful tower without its spire.

(Above) Little Trinity on King Street, the oldest church building in Toronto.

Day One for Toronto was March 6, 1834 when the name of the town of York, Upper Canada was changed to Toronto. Day One for pipe organs is less certain. We know that a fine pipe organ was installed in St. James' Church in 1837 and was lost in the fire of 1839. We also know that a one-manual Mead organ was installed in St. James' in 1842 and that it exists, restored and playable, in the gallery at St. Clement's, Eglinton. Of even more certain origin is the 1847 barrel organ in the gallery of St. John's, York Mills. It played thirty hymn tunes with the turning of a crank in a candle-lit brick church built in 1844. Damaged during its journey from England, the barrel organ was repaired by John Thomas, a 'Builder of Pianofortes and Organs' at Harmony Place, 140 King Street West. It is still playable, and stands in the gallery at St. John's. The honour of being first may, after all, turn out to be a house organ loaned to St. James' in the early 1830s for music that needed an organ.

1850–1900

In 1849, John Thomas installed an organ in the gallery of the north transept of the new Holy Trinity Church (1847). The population of Toronto numbered 20,000 and to the north of the cleared area around the church were forest and a few buildings up Yonge Street. The organ "was blown by hand by one who received for his services two shillings and sixpence a month."[1]

An east-end and a west-end church had already opened to take the load off St. James' Cathedral which had 6,000 members by 1844 but seats for only 1,500. Trinity Episcopal Church (Little Trinity) opened on February 14, 1844 on King Street near Parliament and St. George the Martyr on November 9, 1845 on John Street north of Queen Street. The first organ at St. George the Martyr "was in the centre of the west gallery. It was replaced by another in 1857, which was moved to the south of the chancel in 1876. Built by Warren of Montreal, at a cost of $2,500.00, it was rebuilt and enlarged by Warren & Son of Toronto in 1880 at an additional cost of $1,500.00. The instrument was pumped by hand, and it is recorded that the sexton received $24.00 per annum for this extra duty. A water motor was installed in 1881, the gift of Mrs. Charles J. Rose, wife of the organist of that time."[2]

The 1857 Warren Great Organ was still in place when I became organist at St. George's in 1953. The trackers were connected to electro-pneumatic pull-downs and the 3 manual organ had a draw knob console built in 1935. The Great chorus was complete with principals 8, 4, 2-2/3, 2 and a 3-rank mixture plus a trumpet 8'. The trumpet was unusual in that it had parallel, beveled-end shallots with tongues that were wider at the wedge than at the tip so the tone was intense and brilliant like nothing I had ever heard except perhaps on the recordings of Albert Schweitzer playing the Silberman organ in Gunsbach, Alsace. For the rebuilding of the organ in the Eaton shop in 1955 I made new tongues as copies of the old. Not many heard the organ and the Choir Organ was never finished. Early one Sunday morning in February 1951 a phone call came from an elderly member of the choir and I heard words I shall never forget, "Mr. Jackson. Our church is on fire."

The fire at St. George the Martyr began in the furnace room and burned out the floor in the choir room but missed the gowns in the cupboards. The organ was destroyed except for one rank of Lieblich Bourdon pipes which had been stored in the parish hall. These lovely wooden pipes from the organ of 1880 are now in the Great Organ of the Eaton-Morel Organ in Queen Street United Church, Lindsay. The congregation of St. George's first moved into the old Rectory where a two-stop, one-manual Eaton Organ was installed. Later, they moved the worship space to the parish hall and had the organ, with one stop added, placed on a movable platform. The bell tower is all that remains of the church. Two rows of trees were planted to mark the position of the pillars in the nave.

Until the turn of the century, in most churches, it took two to play the organ, one to work the pump handle and one to play the keys. It took three to tune the organ. The exceptions were organs blown by water

power. There remains to this day a water motor in the tower of St. Michael's Cathedral.

In the late 1840s Edward Lye arrived from Somerset, England, and found work in a furniture factory.[3] In 1864 he began building small tracker action organs and by 1900 built over 170 organs of which 70 were installed in

The water motor installed in 1880 to blow the S. R. Warren Organ in St. Michael's Cathedral. It operated on fifty pounds of water pressure. The large diameter pipe is a drain pipe. The large rod at the top is driven by a double-acting piston and is connected to a rocking lever and two 'feeder bellows'.

Toronto. His Opus 16 was built for Trinity Episcopal Church (Little Trinity) in about 1871; in the late 1890s a second organ Opus 202 was built with pneumatic action.

The first organ by S. R. Warren of Montreal arrived about 1853. Many important instruments such as the Gallery organs for St. James' Cathedral of 1853, St. Michael's Cathedral of 1880 and St. Andrew's Presbyterian Church of 1884 were built by Samuel Russel Warren. The firm's name changed in 1876 to S. R. Warren & Son when Warren was joined by his son Charles Summer Warren.

A few other builders left their mark on the city, most notably R. S. Williams of Oshawa and Toronto, who built the two-manual tracker organ in St. Paul's Basilica on Power Street.

This half-century seemed to belong to Edward Lye for the small churches and Warren for the larger ones. D. W. Karn of Woodstock moved in later in the mid

xiv

1880s and merged with Warren in 1896 as Karn-Warren and together built the very large organ in Metropolitan United Church.

Alas, the hundreds of organs from this period were soon to disappear. The little tracker organs were built of solid, local lumber, probably air dried and placed in

The S. R. Warren organ of 1884 in St. Andrew's Presbyterian Church.

churches subject to more and more heating as the years went by. Windchests split and notes ran together as the wood sliders became loose. Other sliders would stick and stops became hard to draw. Actions would go out of adjustment and needed expert maintenance which was not always available. Wealthy city congregations could afford coal which heated and cooked the organs, but they could also afford to replace instruments that became troublesome. These simple instruments had none of the features such as floating fulcrums, frictionless squares and slider seals which make the later 20th century mechanical action organs so reliable and sensitive to play. By the end of the 20th century the only remaining Lye Organs were in country churches. A 10 stop, Lye organ Opus 170, in St. James' Anglican Church, Caledon East was moved in 1948 from St. Cyprian's Church, Toronto. Two examples of original installations of Edward Lye & Sons organs are in Christ Church, Bailieboro and in St. Thomas' Anglican Church in Millbrook.

If tracker action would not work well enough, neither did many organs with tubular action. Introduced in the early 1880s, tubular pneumatic action was touted as a means of overcoming heavy key action and making it possible to detach consoles. A slight change of pressure at the end of long tubes of soft, bendable lead, one per note, was used to move a small primary valve which in turn moved a larger secondary one which exhausted an air channel cut across the width of the wind chest. Thus twenty stops could be played as easily as two. The aural response, however, was slow and the tactile connection was lost.

Many different stop actions and key note actions were devised. D. W. Karn was so inventive that it was unusual to find two organs with the same windchest action. Unfortunately Karn used a method of construction for the windchests which fastened thick top boards to the chest wells and dividing rails with the wood grain running crossways. The dry winters caused leaks in the pneumatic system. Most were difficult to maintain and none were suitable for lasting restoration.

Electro-pneumatic action held promise but was still in the developmental stage in the early 1890s. Tubular-pneumatic action remained in production through the 1920s but was reserved for smaller instruments.

1900-1950

The turning point for the Toronto organ scene was 1904 when a two-manual, Casavant tubular pneumatic action organ was installed at the Church of the Redeemer at Avenue Road and Bloor Street. Here at last was an organ that would survive the winter cooking and summer humidity. It is said that the father, Joseph Casavant, built a kiln to dry lumber pulled from the forest. He learned how to build for the fiercely cold conditions of Quebec. The sons, Claver and Samuel, had the added advantage of travel overseas where they experienced the new and old tone of the organs of Europe. By 1904 the Casavant brothers, established in 1879, had built over 200 organs, developed electro-pneumatic action (1890) and applied it to Ventil-type windchests.

Claver Casavant at the console of the organ in the Royal York Hotel.

In 1907 they installed the four-manual, 46-stop, electro-pneumatic action organ in St. Andrew's Presbyterian Church on King Street and made electro-pneumatic pull-down action to play much of the 1884 Warren semi-tracker organ in the gallery from the new console in the chancel. Five organs were installed by Casavant in Toronto the next year, including the four-manual, 60-stop organ in Walmer Road Baptist Church. When their Opus 550 was installed in 1914 in St. Paul's Church on Bloor Street, it was said to be the fifth largest organ in the world. Electro-pneumatic action was used for the large instruments. An extra charge was made to use electric instead of pneumatic action.

The roaring twenties had a special meaning for Toronto as more and larger organs arrived. In 1928 the newly built Yorkminster Baptist Church received the four-manual, 80-stop organ donated by Lieutenant Governor Albert and Mrs. Matthews. The next year the Royal York Hotel installed the five-manual 92-stop Casavant Opus 1312 in the Concert Hall. Of similar specification but slightly and deliberately larger by two stops, Opus 1367 was installed at Metropolitan United Church in 1930. At the end of this remarkable era, the Eatons had Opus 1414 of four manuals and 78 stops installed in Eaton Auditorium on the 7th floor of Eaton's College Street store. The Royal York Hotel organ was used very little, but the Eaton organ was frequently

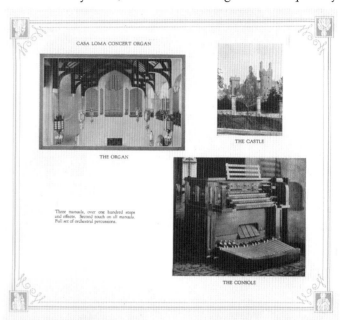

(Above) A page from a C. Franklin Legge residence organ catalogue showing the three manual Unit organ later moved to the CKNC Studios *(left)* on Davenport Road and then to CBC Studio 'G' on Jarvis Street. The Great Hall of Casa Loma now houses a Wurlitzer 'Unit Orchestra' from Shea's Hippodrome. It was installed there by the Toronto Theatre Organ Society and is used regularly for concerts.

played. A branch of the Casavant Society was formed in 1938. Founding members included Lady Eaton, Lady Kemp and Sir Ernest MacMillan. Many prominent organists played concerts, including Glen Gould who made his debut as an organist during the 1945 series.

Regrettably, both the Eaton Auditorium and the Royal York organs are no longer in Canada and have been installed in churches in the U.S.A.. When Eaton's College Street store was sold to a developer, a controversy developed over the ownership of the organ. It was given to Evangel Temple for use in their new church in Hogg's Hollow, provided it was removed from the hall before closing date for sale of the Eaton store. On March 24, 1977, after four weeks of dismantling and packing by a crew of five Casavant builders, the fifth 40-foot transport truck left for Acton, Ontario, where the organ was stored for seven years. It was then bought by Edgar Morrison and installed by Keates-Geissler Pipe Organs Ltd. in First Baptist Church, Dallas, ostensibly donated as a tribute to Mr. Morrison's mother. The $490,000 paid by the church was to result in an instrument with a replacement value of $1.6 million.[5] A similar deal followed when the Royal York organ went to First Baptist Church, Jackson, Mississippi. Other schemes with southern Baptist churches eventually led to an investigation by the FBI. Mr. Morrison was arrested in 1991 in Orillia by the RCMP, extradited to the U.S.A. and jailed on charges of fraud.

Other builders installing organs in Toronto were the Woodstock Pipe Organ Builders who also built electro-pneumatic-action organs with Ventil wind chests. Many of these organs remain in use. They are serviceable and can usually be rebuilt. Other contracts went to L. E. Morel who came out of the Casavant shop to Toronto in 1904 as a salaried agent, and then began building organs on his own. The Depression years fostered a low-cost trade in pipe organs. For over twenty years the Franklin Legge Organ Company built organs from a Dufferin Street shop. Most were built on the unit system and with pipes from older organs. An elegant catalogue was published by Legge aimed at the residence organ trade. It pictured the case and three-manual console of the organ in Casa Loma. The same console appeared later in the CKNC studios on Davenport Road. The organ was moved to the CBC building on Jarvis Street and installed in Studio 'G', previously the chapel of Havergal College. Programmes of readings by announcer Austin Willis were accompanied by the famous theatre organist, Quentin Maclean, who also played a Wurlitzer each afternoon at Shea's Hippodrome Theatre on Bay Street and was organist at Holy Rosary Church on St. Clair Avenue.

Concerts in Toronto in 1948 would always begin with 'God Save the King'. Muriel Gidley (Stafford) who played the next organ recital at Eaton Auditorium on December 1, 1948 recalls that Sir Ernest used the organ's snare drum to lead into the National Anthem.

Shea's Hippodrome was a large theatre on Bay Street on the west side of the old City Hall. Long after sound films were invented, the Wurlitzer Organ was played daily by the organist Quentin Maclean. In about 1949 I worked for many weeks with old-timer Jim Dawson re-leathering the chest actions. Each morning we opened a cell and closed off the wind supply and left a note for Mr. Maclean to say what stops would be silent that day. There was never any music on the music desk, just names of tunes or the notes of a tune. We climbed the steel stairways through a forest of hemp rope and pulleys and went through a soundproof hatch into one of the two concrete-lined chambers set high on either side of the theatre. Sharply at 2 p.m. the organ wind came on with a great whump and the music would start, or at least half the music as 9 of the 18 ranks of pipes were in the opposite chamber. The wind regulators would shake with the tremulants, the shutters flip open and closed, and the heavy pressure caused each bass note from the 16' Pedal Tibias to give one a punch in the chest. For two weeks we heard excerpts from Bizet's Carmen. Other times it was hit tunes of the day. "Buttons and Bows" was one which dates this experience. The music was loud but beautiful. Quentin Maclean was classically trained as a cathedral organist and could play the major works of J. S. Bach from memory. The Wurlitzer organ spent a few years in Maple Leaf Gardens and now forms part of the organ in Casa Loma.

Residence organs were installed by the hundreds in the homes of the wealthy across North America before the Great Depression. The Aeolian Company was the main supplier. In Toronto owners of Aeolian Organs included Howard Seagram and Lady Eaton. Automatic players were an important feature of such instruments. The three-manual 1933 Casavant organ from the R. Y. Eaton home went to Little Trinity Church, King Street East and was installed in the gallery by David Legge. It replaced the Edward Lye Organ, Opus 202, which was lost in the fire of 1960.

By the end of the half century the Second World War was over and change was in the air. Woodstock Organs closed. The Legge shop closed and was bought by the T. Eaton Company which built organs for 13 years. Most of these instruments used pipes from old tracker and pneumatic organs, in some cases instruments replaced by electronic organs sold by Eaton's piano department.

The Casavant furniture division, which had helped the firm through the Depression years, stood ready to

expand in case electronic organs took away the business. In Europe, however, Albert Schweitzer's "back to the organ of Bach" movement was under way.

1950-2000

A flood of new organs arrived from Casavant  during the 1950's, two or three per year including Kew Beach United 3/35 Opus 2030 and Kingston Road United 3/29 Opus 2043 in 1950, Humbercrest United 3/29 Opus 2093 in 1951, Kingsway Lambton United 3/37 Opus 2211 in 1954 and First Church of Christ, Scientist 3/49 Opus 2343 in 1956. The tone and specifications were a continuation of the Orchestral-English organs of the previous three decades except that stops from the classic period began to appear in name if not in tonal style. The organ for the new "Gothic" chapel at Trinity College Casavant 2/24 Opus 2274, 1956 displayed a case with carved pipe shades and the stop list contained mutations and mixture work.

Then in 1959 the first "reformed" organ arrived at Forest Hill United Church with low pressure un-nicked pipework all exposed to view and without expression shutters. It was a Bach organ in tone and intent though it did not have mechanical key or stop action, a prerequisite in the design of the reformed organ. The following year, the large classic style Casavant Opus 2589 of 4 divisions, 59 stops was installed in All Saints' Kingsway Church. For a number of years a monthly recital series called *Le Grand Orgue* was played there by RCCO National

Executive members Gordon Jeffery playing Bach and Barrie Cabena playing romantic and modern works. The concerts were a repeat of Aeolian Hall Concerts played in London, Ontario the night before. In 1965 All Saints' Church burned and the organ was totally destroyed.

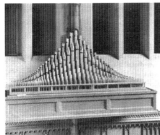

(Opposite) Forest Hill United Church exposed organ.

(Above, and left) The 1960, three-manual, four division, Casavant Organ in All Saints Kingsway Church had a Positif Organ cantilevered from the chancel wall. During the fire in 1965, Rita Chalmers, wife of organist Jim Chalmers saw the Positif through the front door of the church as it toppled into the flames.

In that same year, 1965, a project instigated by a young priest, Rev. John Mott from Our Lady of Sorrows Church, a few blocks to the west of All Saints', became a reality. A two-manual, 25-stop, modern, encased mechanical action Casavant organ was installed. If the clear, exposed sound of the Forest Hill organ was a shock to Toronto organists, the reappearance of mechanical action was a complete surprise to many. The fact that Rudolph von Beckerath had already installed three important tracker organs in Montreal[6] was seemingly unnoticed by the majority of Toronto organists. One exception is organist William Wright who convinced his church of the need to build a better organ for Deer Park United Church. A donor, Charles Rathgeb, provided the funds outright and in advance, and the three-manual, 48-stop tracker-action organ, Casavant Opus 3095, was installed in 1970. For the next thirty years an impressive number of well-known organists were presented in concert. The 1970 season began with Marie Claire Alain, included Mireille Lagacé and concluded with Wilhelm Krumbach. Later years presented Lionel Rogg, André Isoir and one of the last performances by E. Power Biggs who was suffering from arthritis. Biggs had arranged for felt to be inserted under the manual keyboards for the occasion to reduce the travel of the keys. It did not allow the couplers to connect, but his style of playing did not need them.

Organ building slowed during the energy crisis and recession of the early 1970s. Nevertheless a number of new mechanical action organs were installed. At the University of Toronto's Edward Johnson Building, Casavant Opus 3185, 2/25 was installed in 1973 in Walter Hall. Casavant's newly arrived Tonal Director was Gerhard Brunzema from Leer, Germany. The partnership of Ahrend and Brunzema had been dissolved in

January 1972. The simple squared lines of the casework, small horizontal plaquettes on the pipe shades and the stop list were similar to the most recent work of Ahrend and Brunzema such as the 1970 organ in the Church Cantate Domino, Frankfurt-Nordwestadt. The simple case style may also be seen on the 1981, two-manual 20-stop tracker organ, Casavant Opus 3534, at St. Bonaventure's Church in Don Mills. We are told that Brunzema had a saying for organ builders: "Where the curve begins, the profit ends."

Other instruments representing the reformed organ style are at Rosedale Presbyterian Church, two manuals, 20 stops by Karl Wilhelm, built in 1982 and at Christ Church, Deer Park, also by Karl Wilhelm. In 1988 the two-manual, 20-stop Casavant tracker action organ was installed at the Church of the Annunciation. In 1989 the first Hellmuth Wolff organ in Toronto was installed in a new gallery in Knox College Chapel, an organ with modified mean-tone tuning designed as a teaching instrument. The scaling and stop list are based on a 17th century Cahman organ in the Leufsta Bruk in Sweden.

In 1997 the Church of the Holy Family was destroyed by fire and the two-manual, 20-stop tracker organ, built ten years earlier in the Brunzema shop in Fergus, Ontario, was lost. A three-manual, Gabriel Kney tracker action organ of 49 stops from the residence of the Late Gordon Jeffery has been installed by Halbert Gober in the new church.

In September 1982, Roy Thomson Hall was opened with a new four-manual, 71-stop Gabriel Kney mechanical action organ in place. The very next year in September 1983 a new three-manual, 50-stop Karl Wilhelm mechanical action organ was installed at St. Andrew's Presbyterian Church across the street.

The organs chosen most frequently for concert programmes in recent years have been Yorkminster Park Baptist, St. Paul's Anglican, St. James' Cathedral and Deer Park United Church. Toward the close of the century the emerging concert venues were Lawrence Park Community Church, Timothy Eaton Memorial Church, and St. Clement's Anglican Church, with its rebuilt organ.

It would be presumptuous to predict what the next half century will bring to the Toronto organ scene. It is certain that organ builders generally have a better backlog of orders for new instruments than they have had since the 1960s. The caliber of playing of the young organists has progressed to amazing levels. The quality of construction and beauty of tone of the newest organs is far better than it was in 1900 or in 1950. These facts are not indicative of something in decline.

The organ is still the King of Instruments and there is no other musical instrument that has such a stirring effect on people.

Alan Jackson
Toronto, May 2002

1. *The Church of the Holy Trinity*, C. Ian P. Tate, 1965
2. *The Story of the Church of St. George the Martyr*, Harman and Upshall
3. *Encyclopedia of Music in Canada*, page 567
4. *Ibid*, page 164
5. *Hamilton Spectator*, November 29, 1988
6. Queen Mary Road United, 2/26, February 26, 1959;
Oratoire Ste Joseph, 5/78, 1960;
Immaculée-Conception, 3/38, 1961.

Organs of Toronto

CHURCH OF THE ANNUNCIATION

3 Combermere Drive
Casavant Organ Opus 3646, 1988

The choir of the Church of the Annunciation used to sit in aural isolation in the corner where the Pedal Soubasse 16' now stands.

Constructed in 1964, The Church of the Annunciation of the Blessed Virgin Mary represents the influence of the Second Vatican Ecumenical Council of Pope John XXIII on church architecture. The Council re-emphasized the centrality of the mass to worship when it said that the mass is "the summit toward which the activity of the church is directed; it is also the fount from which all her power flows."

Vatican II also sought the restoration of active participation in the liturgy by all the gathered faithful. It recognized the importance of scripture in the celebration of the liturgy, as well as the rite of baptism. Article 120 of the Constitution on the Sacred Liturgy of December 4, 1963 reads "The pipe organ is to be held in high esteem in the Latin Church, for it is the traditional musical instrument, the sound of which can add a wonderful splendor to the Church's ceremonies and powerfully lifts up men's minds to God and higher things."

The form selected for the Church of the Annunciation is one which brings worshippers in close proximity to the liturgy. The plan is a square from which one corner has been truncated in order to provide an atrium or narthex area. At the corner opposite this point of entrance is located the sanctuary. The baptismal font is placed on the central aisle which follows the diagonal of the square and bisects the semi-circular arrangement of pews around the sanctuary. In the sanctuary is an imposing carved altar behind which, on a raised dais, are chairs for those presiding. The altar is complemented by an ambo. The roofline rises as it approaches the altar. In the two walls embracing the sanctuary are set hundreds of small stained glass panels which present an abstract starburst of coloured light – yellows and reds in the centre moving towards deep purples, blues and greens at the edges.

The architecture speaks in the language of its own time: concrete frame, pre-cast concrete wall system, glue-laminated roof beams, vinyl flooring. It is a symbol of the assembly of the community, and underlines the sanctity of the liturgy, baptism and the word.

In 1988 the church installed a new organ. It stands to one side of the sanctuary, against a wall. The top portion of the case, the Grand Orgue and Pédale, rises in three steps from left to right, matching the slope of the roof structure. The Récit is below the Grand Orgue, and just above the music desk. The Pédale Soubasse 16' is set into a recess behind the main case.

Reformed and matured, this organ has all the requirements of the Organ Reform Movement, namely, low pressure, un-nicked pipework, classical choruses of principals and flutes, mechanical key-and-stop action, and encasement. Unlike earlier reformed organs, it has an expressive division and a céleste obtained economically by using flutes instead of the usual pair of strings.

Ultimately it is the curtain of stained glass behind the sanctuary and this well-integrated organ case which visually "make" the room, complemented by the worshippers, as colourful as the wall of stained glass, actively participating in the liturgy.

Casavant Organ Opus 3646, 1988

GRAND ORGUE		FEET	PIPES
1	Montre	8	56
2	Flûte à cheminée	8	56
3	Prestant	4	56
4	Flûte à fuseau	4	56
5	Nazard	2-2/3	56
6	Quarte de nazard	2	56
7	Tierce	1-3/5	56
8	Fourniture IV	1-1/3	224
9	Trompette	8	56

RÉCIT (ENCLOSED)			
10	Bourdon	8	56
11	Bourdon céleste (TenC)	8	44
12	Flûte conique	4	56
13	Doublette	2	56
14	Cymbale III	2/3	168
15	Hautbois (1–12 Half L)	8	56
	Tremblant		

PÉDALE			
16	Soubasse	16	32
17	Octavebasse	8	32
18	Octave	4	32
19	Basson (half-length)	16	32

COUPLERS (MECHANICAL)
Grand Orgue/Pédale
Récit/Pédale
Récit/Grand Orgue

REVERSIBLE PISTONS
Grand Orgue / Pédale   Toe
Récit/Pédale   Toe
Récit/Grand Orgue   Toe

ACTION
Mechanical key and stop action.

CHRIST CHURCH, DEER PARK

1570 Yonge Street
Karl Wilhelm Inc. Organ, 1982

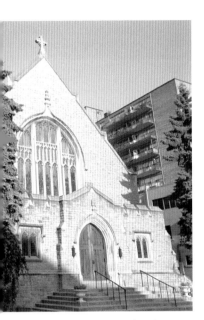

The Parish of Christ Church Deer Park has worshipped, since 1922, in a building located north of Heath Street on the west side of Yonge Street.

The origins of Christ Church, Deer Park go back to the middle of the 19th century. Anglicans living in the area between St. Paul's Church, Bloor Street and St. John's, York Mills, had the choice between a trip southwards or northwards. Ultimately it was the third Rector of St. John's who established a mission in Leaside which then moved to a brick school house at Davisville and Yonge. This became known as the Davisville Mission.

A meeting held on June 6, 1870 decided to ask the Bishop of Toronto to create a new parish. The Bishop and diocese agreed, and a building committee was formed. A site was purchased and a new wood-frame church, complete with a driving shed, was ready for use by Christmas of the same year.

The area was strictly rural. The City of Toronto had just crossed the second concession at Bloor Street by the annexation of Yorkville, but at St. Clair Avenue, the third concession, much of the land continued to be held in large country estates. A portion of the 200-acre farm deeded by the government to Frederick Baron de Hoen, a German nobleman who fought with Britain in the American Revolution, had passed, by 1836, to Agnes Heath. Mrs. Heath was a woman of considerable social standing who had managed to marry both a son and a daughter to children of D'Arcy Boulton Jr. of the Grange, located just south of what is now the Art Gallery of Ontario. She named her new property Deer Park Farm because the family kept a herd of tame deer on the property.

In the 1880s, a tax exemption for lawns and gardens was repealed. This encouraged many of the holders of large estates to begin to subdivide, and the population of the Village of Deer Park began to blossom. By 1909, Christ Church, Deer Park, had outgrown its wood-frame building so work began on a larger, brick replacement.

This second building did not serve the congregation many years before its site was required by the City of Toronto for the widening of Yonge Street from Heath Street to the city limits. The church and property were sold to the City in 1922 and a new site was purchased at the corner of Heath Street and Lawton Boulevard. A design for the new church building, by architects George Moorehouse and King, was presented in

March of the same year, and this building was ready for worship on Easter Day, April 1, 1923.

Christ Church Deer Park is a Neo-Gothic church, in a Late Gothic Revival style, rendered in Owen Sound sandstone with Indiana sandstone detailing, including window tracery. The nave is column-free thanks to an intricate hammer-beam roof structure. Six years later, the same architects achieved similar results at Yorkminster Baptist Church, just across Yonge Street, by using steel trusses.

In 1980, Matsui Baer Vanstone Freeman provided architectural expertise for a complex process which moved the altar to the front of the chancel area, prepared for the installation of the new encased Karl Wilhelm organ where the original altar had been, and placed the choir on chairs arranged in a triple arc to each side of the organ. A large cross hangs over the new altar placement.

An early Edward Lye organ, Opus 34, was built for "Christ's Episcopal Church, Deer Park" on Yonge Street in about 1880. The organ would have been installed in the wood frame church. Then Lye rebuilt the organ as Opus 143 about the same time as the organ for St. Clement's, some time before 1897. Casavant Organ Opus 737 was built in 1918 for the second church. It had 23 stops, 20 ranks and tubular pneumatic action. The organ was moved to the new church in 1923. In 1949 a new console was built and the organ was electrified. The organ occupied the vestry space on the epistle side of the chancel which was large enough to contain the organ and leave a passage behind. The organ was moved by Ross Dodington in 1981 and installed in St. Wilfrid's Anglican Church in Islington.

The encased, Classic-style Karl Wilhelm tracker action organ in Christ Church Deer Park. The altar can be rolled aside and the platform cleared for concert performances.

Karl Wilhelm Inc., 1982

HAUPTWERK

#		
1	Bourdon	16
2	Prinzipal	8
3	Hohlflöte	8
4	Oktave	4
5	Spitzflöte	4
6	Quinte	2-2/3
7	Superoktave	2
8	Mixtur V	1-1/3
9	Cornet V (mid. c)	8
10	Trompete	8

POSITIF

#		
11	Gedackt	8
12	Prinzipal	4
13	Rohrflöte	4
14	Nazard	2-2/3
15	Doublette	2
16	Terz	1-3/5
17	Larigot	1-1/3
18	Scharf III	1
19	Cromorne	8
	Tremolo	

SCHWELLWERK (ENCLOSED)

#		
20	Dolkan	8
21	Rohrflöte	8
22	Celeste	8
23	Prinzipal	4
24	Flöte	4
25	Nachthorn	2
26	Mixtur IV	2
27	Dulzian	16
28	Oboe	8
	Tremolo	

PEDAL

#		
29	Subbass	16
30	Oktavbass	8
31	Pommer	8
32	Choralbass	4
33	Rauschpfeife III	2
34	Posaune	16
35	Trompete	8
36	Clairon	4

COUPLERS
Hauptwerk, Positif, Schwellwerk
  to Pedal
Positif, Schwellwerk to Pedal
Schwellwerk to Positif

ACTION
Mechanical key and stop action

CONVOCATION HALL

University of Toronto, King's College Circle
Casavant Organ Opus 474, 1911
New console and additions 1929

One of the great revelations of the research for this book has been the generally clear decisions and quick action which seemed to be associated with the construction or rebuilding of many of our historic churches. Some appeared to have been conceived in the spring and in use by Christmas.

The story of Convocation Hall does not fit this mold. As early as 1886, there was discussion related to building a new Convocation Hall, made more necessary after the first Convoctaion Hall was destroyed by fire in 1890. Transfer of the old King's College building to the government provided the wherewithal to build a new hall. In a letter to the Editors of *The Varsity*, a Wm. Houston suggested that the architects should be instructed to provide accommodation for an organ.

The editor of *The Varsity* of February 25, 1903 noted that "it must be a noble piece of architecture; it must be spacious; it must be provided with fine mural decorations and an organ. It must, in a word, provide for, encourage and develop the aesthetic side of student nature."

It was the alumni of the Provincial University who took it upon themselves to gather the required funding for a new hall. Their campaign emphasized the need for a good public auditorium for audiences not large enough to fill Massey Hall (c.1890). Architects Darling & Pearson were selected and a design approved by the Executive Council of the University Alumni Association in March 1904.

(Opposite) For close to a century students of the University of Toronto, their proud parents, and friends have been attending graduating exercises in Convocation Hall and since 1912 have processed to the tones of its Casavant Organ.

Convocation Hall opened in June of 1907 at a cost of $230,000, some $180,000 more than anticipated, the shortfall being picked up by the Province of Ontario. The design is classical in inspiration, in the lineage of the Beaux-Arts movement. For its time, the Ionic-columned circular hall was a return to simpler forms than those in vogue at the height of Gothic Revival and other picturesque styles.

By 1925 critics were bemoaning the aesthetics of the hall. *The Varsity* of November 24, 1925 records that "it is argued that a hall for Convocation and other great ceremonies should have been a hall of the Gothic type and not an auditorium." The choice of style and cheaper materials was explained as having been driven by budget constraints.

Convocation Hall is a circular auditorium seating 1,500 on a main level, in an amphitheatred dress circle, and on a total of 14 balconies set into seven alcoves around the room. The organ case, with its flats of pipes between two large towers and three smaller ones, is supported on a shelf set into an eighth niche behind the raised platform area. The central portion of the ceiling is a large, opalescent glass oculus through which daylight floods the hall. Plaster ribs radiating from a plaster frame around this opening align with each column.

The circular shape, of course has presented some acoustical problems, and, due to the many niches, the room does not provide the reverberation desirable for much of the organ repertoire. The niches always did trap sound, but in later years the ceiling surface in each alcove was covered with sound-absorptive material which further reduced the reverberation time. Drapes and carpet installed in 1925 had already deadened the acoustic in the Hall. Once dead, the most serious flaw was intensified as a distinct repetition of sound which can be heard anywhere near the centre of the floor area, a clear echo from the curved dome above.

In November 1908 an initial, unofficial inquiry was made to the "Casavant Brothers" for a design for "a really fine concert and recital organ, which would also be used for leading the singing during the University

The installation of the Convocation Hall organ, January 1912. On the left is the double-decked expression box for the Swell Organ above and the Choir below. On the right is the Solo expression box. In the centre is the Great Organ with the upper Great chest suspended from block and tackle while the crew pauses for the photographer.

10

sermons."[1] The Warren Church Organ Co. of Woodstock was also approached and responded with a quotation.

In 1910 an official request for quotes was sent out, this time by the Bursar, Mr. F. A. Mouré, and a proposal was obtained from the Karn-Morris Piano & Organ Company of Woodstock and from four English builders as well as Casavant. In their new proposal in November 1910, the brothers quoted $15,000 stating that it would "give you a very fine instrument but the hall can stand a still larger organ if money is not a consideration." The Bursar replied by asking what the builder would recommend, but added, "We do not want an instrument that will be the largest of its kind or that will be too heavy for the building." The recommended organ of 69 stops was to cost $16,150.00 plus $2,050.00 for casework. The organ "would surely make a magnificent instrument both tonally and mechanically. Special attention would be given to the Diapasons and Reeds which would be made after the best and most modern of English voicing."[2] Prices were included for four types of bells "as opinions and tastes differ." The organ was built with Cathedral Chimes and a Célesta of 4 octaves imported from Metzler & Co. of London, a dealer in "all kinds of Wind, Reed and Stringed Instruments, Toy Instruments, Musical Boxes." The Célestas were probably made in Paris by Mustel and were fitted with electro-pneumatic pull-down actions built by Casavant. These instruments were also installed in the organs at St. Paul's, Bloor Street, St Andrew's Evangelical Lutheran, and St. Paul's, Avenue Road. The new organ was ready to be shipped by January 1912, but was delayed one week to make changes because the height available for the 32' pipes was reduced with the installation of a false ceiling after the loft had been measured. The organ was first played in recital in June 1912.

In 1929 the old terraced console was replaced with a new four-manual Casavant console of "English" type. Also added were 12 pipes to extend the Trombone 16' to 32' pitch, a new Choir Trumpet 8', a Deagan Harp of 61 notes and a French Horn 8' for the Solo. The Solo expression box was increased in height. The new console was installed in the same position as the original, centre stage but too close to the organ case. This has meant that organists and tuners have never been able to hear properly what they were playing. The problem was made worse in later years when the carpet, drapes and acoustic materials were installed. By the end of the century, despite the tonal improvements of 1980, the organ was being used for convocations and student practice but rarely for the concerts envisioned by Mssrs. Abbott and Mouré.

1 Letter from Albert H. Abbott, Casavant Archives.
2 Letter of Samuel Casavant.

ORIGINS, ADDITIONS

1912   Organ installed beginning January and opened June 6, 1912

1929   Contract signed May 18 for a new console and additional stops and a larger expression box over the Solo.

1929   October 1929 additions completed.

1968   Solo Organ reservoir leathering burst, releathering of main reservoirs begun.

1978   Began major overhaul and tonal revisions, console repairs, action re-leathering, cleaning, work completed April 1980.

1994   Began progressive conversion of the main windchests to Pitman action and schwimmer winding, Console converted to electric drive and solid-state switching and combinations.

Covocation Hall
(*Continued*)

Casavant Organ Opus 474, 1911
New console and additions 1929
Tonal revisions 1980

*new pipes 1980
†new tongues 1980

Grand Orgue		Feet	Pipes
1	Montre	16	61
2	Bourdon	16	61
3	Montre	8	61
4	Principal	8	61
5	Flûte	8	61
6	Flûte Harmonique	8	61
7	Cor de Chamois	8	61
8	Octave	4	61
9	Prestant	4	61
10	Flûte Octaviante	4	61
11	Quinte	2-2/3	61
12	Doublette	2	61
13*	Fourniture	V	305
14*	Cymbale	IV	244
15*	Cornet (TC)	II	98
16†	Bombarde	16	61
17†	Trompette	8	61
	Harp		

Récit (enclosed)			
18	Bourdon	16	61
19	Principal	8	61
20	Flûte Ouverte	8	61
21	Gedackt	8	61
22	Viole de Gambe	8	61
23	Voix Céleste (TC)	8	49
24	Dulciane	8	61
25	Fugara	4	61
26	Flûte Traversiere	4	61
27	Piccolo	2	61
28*	Plein jeu	V	305
29*	Cornet (TC)	III	147
30†	Basson	16	61
31†	Trompette	8	61
32	Hautbois	8	61
33	Voix Humaine	8	61
34†	Clairon	4	61
	Tremblant		

Positif			
35	Salicional	8	61
36	Bourdon	8	61
37	Gambe	8	61
38	Prestant	4	61
39	Flûte Ouverte	4	61
40	Nazard	2-2/3	61
41	Quarte de Nazard	2	61
42	Tierce	1-3/5	61
43	Larigot	1-1/3	61
44*	Plein jeu	IV-V	293
45†	Basson	16	61
46†	Trompette	8	61
47†	Cromorne	8	61
	Tremulant		
	Harp		

Solo (enclosed)			
48	Flûte à Cheminée	8	61
49	Quintaton	8	61
50	Viole d'Orchestre	8	61
51	Violes Célestes II	8	122
52	Flûte Octaviante	4	61
53	Cor Anglais	8	61
54	Hautbois d'orchestre	8	61
	Tremulant		
55	Célesta	49 actions	

Bombarde (enclosed)			
56	Principal	8	61
57*	Octave	4	61
58	Quinte	2-2/3	61
59*	Octavin	2	61
60*	Fourniture	IV	244
61†	Contre Bombarde	16	61
62†	Bombarde	8	61
63*	Clairon	4	61

64	Harp (1929)	61 actions	
	Harp Sub		
65	Chimes	25 actions	

Pédale			
66	Flûte Ouverte (ext #67) (4 pipes polyphonic)	32	8
67	Flûte Ouverte	16	32
68	Montre	16	32
69	Violon	16	32
70	Bourdon	16	32
71	Dulciane	16	32
72	Bourdon doux (from #18)	16	—
73	Octave	8	32
74	Violoncelle (ext #69)	8	12
75	Bourdon (ext #70)	8	12
76*	Basse de Chorale	4	32
77*	Fourniture	IV	128
78	Contre Bombarde (ext#79) (1929)	32	12
79	Bombarde	16	32
80	Trompette (ext #79)	8	12
81	Clairon (ext #79)	4	12
	Chimes		

Couplers (on tilting tablets)
Grand Orgue, Récit,
    Positif, Solo
    Bombarde à la Pédale 8
Récit, Positif, Solo, Bombarde,
    au Grand Orgue 16, 8, 4
Bombarde, Solo au Récit 8
Récit, Solo au Positif 16, 8, 4
Grand Orgue 16, 4
Récit 16, 4
Positif 16, 8 off, 4
Solo 16, 4
All Swells to Swell Control

Pistons (99 levels, Artisan Classic System)
Grand Orgue 1 2 3 4 5 6   Thumb
Récit   1 2 3 4 5 6   Thumb
Positif   1 2 3 4 5 6   Thumb
Solo   1 2 3   Thumb
Bombarde   1 2 3   Thumb
Pédale   1 2 3 4 5 6
    in G.O. slip duplicated as Toe pistons
General 1 2 3 4 5 6 7 8 9 10 11 12
    In G.O. key slip duplicated as Toe pistons
Adjuster
Release

Reversibles
Grand Orgue, Récit, Positif, Bombarde à la Pédale
Récit, Positif, Bombarde au Grand Orgue
Bombarde au Récit
Récit au Positif
Full organ toe piston
Chimes damper toe Piston
All Swell to Swell toe Pistons

Balanced Pedals
Récit   16 stages
Bombarde, Solo   16 stages
Crescendo

Analysis

	stops	ranks	pipes	real stops
Grand Orgue	17	25	1501	17
Récit	17	23	1355	17
Positif	13	17	1025	13
Solo	8	9	488	8
Bombarde	10	13	671	10
Pédale	15	11	420	8
Totals	80	98	5460	73

DEER PARK UNITED CHURCH

129 St. Clair Avenue West
Casavant Organ Opus 3095, 1970

While Deer Park United's close proximity to the St. Clair streetcar line has been a blessing to worshippers and concert-goers, it has required special considerations during recording sessions.

(Overleaf) The two deeply recessed and widely separated organ chambers at either side of the chancel lie closed as they should. The audiences at the Deer Park United Church Organ Concerts can see the player's hands and feet by sitting left front; can face the organ from the opposite transept or can hear the organ at low volume by sitting under the rear gallery.

The dedication of Deer Park Presbyterian Church in February of 1913 represented the third church building and the second location for a congregation which first met for worship in 1882. From frame construction, to brick, to the Credit Valley greystone of the present church, each reincarnation has borne witness to the increased resources and more demanding tastes of the growing congregation. When this congregation became part of The United Church of Canada at the time of union in 1925, some members chose to remain true to their Calvinistic roots, and established Calvin Presbyterian just a few city blocks to the north.

Deer Park United Church is a building designed in a Late Gothic Revival style by architects Sharp and Brown of Toronto. This style is plainer and less self-conscious than some of the earlier Gothic Revival architecture so plentiful downtown. The plan of the church is cruciform. At the transepts the room is 27 metres (90 feet) in width, and the measurement from the rear of the 11-metre (36 feet) deep balcony to the rear of the chancel is 36.5 metres (120 feet). It is 12 metres (40 feet) to the height of the ceiling. The church was designed to accommodate 1,100 worshippers.

For approximately eighteen years of its life, the original 1913 Casavant Frères Organ, Opus 508, was located behind a pipe screen across the rear of what today is the chancel. In front of the organ were terraced risers for the choir, and, at the alignment of the transepts, a centrally placed pulpit.

In 1931 major renovations, directed by architect A. Mackenzie Brydon, created a divided choir and moved the organ into two Gothic-styled cases mounted on the side walls of the chancel area. In this arrangement a new massive pulpit was provided to the east side, and to the west side a wrought iron lectern.

In an arrangement of new pews, designed more along Art Deco lines than following the Gothic Revival precedents of the room, a central aisle was provided for the first time. Structurally this room remained unchanged, although an octagonally shaped Sunday School room just behind the choir was demolished in order to make way for the spacious social and Christian Education facilities found at Deer Park United today. In 1944, the collapse of a portion of the ceiling necessitated a total

redecoration of the sanctuary, and upon the passing of a well-loved minister of the Church, Dr. G. Stanley Russell, the chancel was renovated as a memorial. It was this remodelling which added an exaggerated chancel arch which effectively hid the organ, and two additional stained glass windows were added to either side of the principal south window.

When the matter of a new organ was raised in the 1960s, the issue of placement was not easily resolved. The two acoustically preferred, axially placed locations, either at the front of the church or on the rear gallery, were equally problematic. A design proposal for the rear location placed the new organ near the gallery rail, on which was mounted a Ruckpositiv. This location greatly reduced the church seating capacity and some members of the congregation felt that the required move of the choir to the gallery level was too "like a number of Roman Catholic churches" and that "this choice of location was becoming outdated."

A proposal by Casavant Frères for a new instrument in the chancel area determined that the confined space (remember the three large windows across the south wall) would greatly limit the organ. A design for an asymmetrical case on the left side of the chancel was drawn but not accepted.

The compromise solution was to place the new organ in the east transept, leaving the choir in the chancel area with the hope that a second accompanying organ could ultimately be financed. For many years this function has been served by a four-stop Klaus Becker portative, owned by William Wright, organist of the church for more than 35 years. The location selected for the new Casavant Frères organ required that the church's "Soldier's Memorial Window" be relocated to a window opening at the rear of the gallery. Funds

for moving the window and for installing steel supports below the floor for the organ were provided by Mr. Charles C. Rathgeb.

The organ was donated to the church by this same Charles C. Rathgeb in memory of his wife, Eileen Elizabeth, who died in September 1967. Mr. Rathgeb himself died in 1969 before the organ was completed. His son, Charles C. Rathgeb, requested that the organ be dedicated to both his parents.

Casavant Organ Opus 3095, 1970

HAUPTWERK

1	Gedacktpommer	16	56
2	Principal	8	56
3	Rohrflöte	8	56
4	Oktav	4	56
5	Offenflöte	4	56
6	Quint	2-2/3	56
7	Oktav	2	56
8	Kornett V Ten. C-c'''	8	185
9	Mixtur VI	1-1/3	336
10	Scharf III	1/2	168
11	Fagot	16	56
12	Trompete	8	56
13	Klarine	4	56

OBERWERK

14	Gedackt	8	56
15	Salizional	8	56
16	Principal	4	56
17	Koppelflöte	4	56
18	Nasat	2-2/3	56
19	Oktav	2	56
20	Blockflöte	2	56
21	Terz	1-3/5	56
22	Quinteflote	1-1/3	56
23	Scharf IV	1	224
24	Zimbel III	1/4	168
25	Krummhorn	8	56
	Tremulant		

SCHWELLWERK (ENCLOSED)

26	Gedacktflöte	8	56
27	Quintadena	8	56
28	Gamba Ten C	8	44
29	Spitzflöte	4	56
30	Prinzipal	2	56
31	Sifflöte	1	56
32	Sesquialtera II Ten C2-2/3		88
33	Kleinmixtur IV	2/3	224
34	Rankett	16	56
35	Vox humana	8	56
	Tremulant		

PEDAL

36	Prinzipal	16	32
37	Subbass	16	32
38	Oktav	8	32
39	Bordun	8	32
40	Choralbass	4	32
41	Rohrpfeife	4	32
42	Nachthorn	2	32
43	Rauschpfeife III	5-1/3	96
44	Mixtur V	2	160
45	Posaune	16	32
46	Fagott	16	32
47	Trompete	8	32
48	Schalmei	4	32

COUPLERS
Hauptwerk/Pedal
Positiv/Pedal
Schwellwerk/Pedal
Positiv/Hauptwerk
Schwellwerk/Hauptwerk
(Schwellwerk/Positiv
preparation only)
(Continued overleaf)

DEER PARK UNITED
(Continued)

ADJUSTABLE COMBINATION PISTONS
SSL electronic capture system
32 modes

Hauptwerk	1 2 3 4 5	Thumb
Positiv	1 2 3 4 5	Thumb
Schwellwerk	1 2 3 4 5	Thumb
Pedal	1 2 3 4 5	Thumb &toe
General	1 2 3 4 5 6 7 8	Thumb & toe
General Cancel		Thumb
Adjuster		

REVERSIBLE PISTONS

Hauptwerk/Pedal	Thumb & toe
Positiv/Pedal	Thumb & toe
Schwellwerk/Pedal	Thumb & toe
Positiv/Hauptwerk	Thumb & toe
Schwellwerk/ Hauptwerk	Thumb & toe
(Schwellwerk/Positiv preparation only)	
Full Organ	Thumb & toe

ACTION
Mechanical key action, electric
    stop action
Mechanical Swell expression
    pedal

ANALYSIS

	STOPS	RANKS	PIPES	REAL STOPS
Hauptwerk	13	24	1249	13
Oberwerk	12	17	952	12
Schwellwerk	10	14	748	10
Pedal	13	19	608	13
Totals	48	74	3557	48

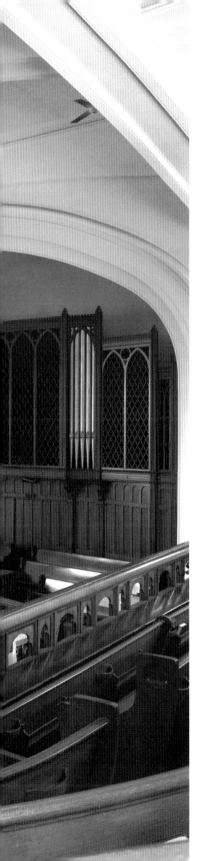

The organ screen of the 1954, M. P. Moller Organ in Eastminster United Church displays ten gilded, wooden dummy pipes. The use of dummy pipes became very rare after the end of the decade.

EASTMINSTER UNITED CHURCH

310 Danforth Avenue
M.P. Moller Inc. Hagerstown, Maryland
Organ Opus 8669, 1954

Eastminister United Church has a very direct historical link to the Prince Edward Viaduct, which joins Danforth Avenue to Bloor Street.

For many years the full development of the Playter land abutting the Second Concession, now Danforth Avenue, was deterred by poor communication across the wide, wet Don flats. The Don Viaduct was first planned in 1903, but only begun in 1915 and finished in 1918.

Danforth Methodist Church had begun meeting in a wood-frame structure in 1907. Construction of a permanent building, on the current site, began three years later. With the new connection to the rest of Toronto, and the end of the First World War, the population of the neighbourhood exploded. When the cornerstone of the present building was laid, the membership of the church was reported to be the largest of any Methodist congregation in the city and the second largest in Canada. The church became a United Church in 1925, and in 1966 took the name Eastminster when it amalgamated with North Broadview United Church. Most recently, Donlands United has joined the two other congregations.

Eastminster United Church is a red-brick building with cut-stone detailing, constructed in a style which can best be described as Collegiate Gothic. The building is very solidly massed and a squat tower anchors the corner of the church nearest the intersection of Danforth and Jackman Avenues.

The main worship space is a distinctly Methodist auditorium, approximately square in plan and rising the equivalent of three stories in height. A balcony rings three sides of the room. On the main level, curved pews on a gently sloped floor follow the front edge of the platform which has been modified over recent years. What would have been a centre pulpit has been rebuilt to one side, placing a communion table in the central location. The choir continues to be arranged in a tiered choir loft facing the congregation. Though not a reverberant space, the room is airy and filled with daylight filtering in through large amber-coloured windows.

The organ is distributed behind the choir, with the console placed to facilitate the organist/conductor. All the speaking stops are behind a speaker cloth screen and a hardwood frame of Gothic inspiration. The ten pipes displayed in front of the screen are, in fact, made of wood and gilded.

Other installations by Moller were the small Unit organ at St. Christopher's Church on-the-Heights, Willowdale, and the three-manual organ, Opus 8964, built in 1956 for Lawrence Park Community Church. It is impressive that in three years the Opus numbers for Moller advanced by 300 organs. The last Moller installation in Toronto was at St. Aidan's Anglican Church where the Moller agent, Mr. Mel Willits of Woodstock, Ontario, installed a three-manual Moller console, and was to rebuild the organ which was a Dawson Brothers instrument. Willits was in financial difficulty by 1963 and was unable to pay for parts needed from Moller. He lost the agency and St. Aidan's lost their down payment.

M.P. Moller Inc. Hagerstown, Maryland
Organ Opus 8669, 1954

GREAT ORGAN		FEET	PIPES
1	Diapason	8	61
2	Bourdon	8	61
3	Octave	4	61
4	Octave Quint	2-2/3	61
5	Super Octave	2	61
6	Mixture	III	183
	Chimes		

SWELL ORGAN (ENCLOSED)			
7	Rohrflote	8	68
8	Viole de Gambe	8	68
9	Viole Celeste Ten C	8	56
10	Principal	4	61
11	Flauto Traverso	4	61
12	Plein Jeu	III	183
13	Trompette	8	68
14	Schalmei	4	68
	Tremulant		

CHOIR ORGAN			
15	Gedeckt	8	68
16	Erzahler	8	68
17	Erzahler Celeste Ten C	8	56
18	Nachthorn	4	61
19	Nazard	2-2/3	61
20	Blockflote	2	61
21	Tierce	1-3/5	61
	Tremulant		

Pedal Organ			
22	Soubasse	16	32
23	Rohrgedeckt (ext #7)	16	12
24	Octave	8	32
25	Bourdon (ext #22)	8	12
26	Rohrflote (from #7)	8	—
27	Super Octave (ext #24)	4	12
28	Bourdon (ext #22)	4	12
29	Octavin (ext #24)	2	12
30	Double Trompette (ext #13)	16	12
31	Trompette (from #13)	8	—

Couplers

Combination Pistons

18

FOREST HILL UNITED CHURCH

2 Wembley Road
Casavant Organ Opus 2553, 1959

Previous to 1959 a Franklin Legge Organ was located in a second floor room on the left side and spoke through a wooden grille just above the present Great Organ. The new Casavant Organ in Forest Hill United Church is entirely unenclosed and speaks on very low wind pressure. Every one of the fourteen stops is in a direct line of hearing with the congregation.

On May 21, 1940, the cornerstone of a new church building was laid for Forest Hill United Church near the intersection of Bathurst Street and Wembly Road. This was followed by a "Service for the Purposes of Constituting a Congregation" at St. James-Bond United Church on Avenue Road, a short distance to the east.

The construction of this new United Church, like several others being built at the time, including Leaside United, Cosburn United, and the former Armour Heights United Churches, was supported by the George H. Armstrong Church Extension Fund.

George Armstrong was born in 1858 and followed a career in teaching with the Toronto Public School Board. For the last thirteen years of his professional life he was one of Toronto's Inspectors of Public Schools. In the early part of the 20th century he served as Sunday School Superintendent of the Carlton Street Primitive Methodist Church, and was a member of its Board of Trustees for much of his life. When he died in 1938, at the age of eighty, he bequeathed the residue of his estate "for the purpose of establishing new churches in the outlying districts or suburbs of Toronto."[1]

Surprisingly, the plans for a new church received opposition from none other than neighbouring churches. Deer Park, Eaton Memorial and the former St. Columba United Churches all submitted letters of protest on the grounds that the new church represented an invasion of their territory.

A design for the new facility by J. Francis Brown and Son, Architects, included both a chapel seating 210 worshippers and a church seating 450. Given the financial constraints of the new congregation, it was decided to proceed with the chapel only, at an estimated cost of between $21,000 and $22,000, available through the Church Extension Fund.

This is the building we see today. With the exception of an additional 7 metres (24 feet) of length to the south to provide a more pleasing entrance, and a few additional pews, the simple Modern Gothic building has remained unchanged. Particularly charming is the steeply-sloped timber roof structure sitting on the low masonry walls. None of these features contribute to a very successful acoustic, but provide an intimacy sought by many a bride.

Almost twenty years after the building was constructed, the provisional C. Franklin Legge electro-pneumatic organ broke down, and the church signed a $14,000 contract with Casavant Frères for an organ which was most unusual for the times. Of course, as pipe organs do, the old Legge Organ played for another eighteen years after it was moved to Northminster United Church on Finch Avenue.

The organist at Forest Hill United Church in 1959 was Earl Moss, a well known piano teacher at the Royal Conservatory. He was aware of the reform taking place in the pipe organ scene and knew how to play the little Bach organ. The console has a "Swell Pedal," but only as a place to rest a foot and maintain balance while playing. There are no reed pipes in the organ, so it can be left without tuning for at least one or two years at a time. A craze to "see the pipes" started with builders such as Holtkamp and Aeolian Skinner and lasted over twenty years in some areas. The little organ loft outside the chancel ceiling, which used to contain the Legge unit organ, served better as a blower room. The action of the new organ is Pitman type, electro-pneumatic and the winding was the first example of schwimmer wind supply in Toronto.

1. Wording as found in the bequest quoted in a brochure produced by the UCC entitled "George N. Armstrong 1858-1938"

Casavant Organ Opus 2553, 1959

GREAT ORGAN (WEST WALL)

1	Gedackt	8	56
2	Principal	4	56
3	Blockflote	2	56
4	Quinteflote	1-1/3	56
5	Mixture III	1	168

POSTIV (EAST WALL)

6	Rohrflote	8	56
7	Spitzflote	4	56
8	Principal	2	56
9	Sesquialtera II	2-2/3	112
10	Zimbel III	1/4	168

PEDAL (NORTH WALL)

11	Subbass	16	32
12	Spitzprincipal	8	32
13	Choralbass	4	32
14	Nachthorn	2	32

COUPLERS
Great to Pedal
Positiv to Pedal
Positiv to Great

COMBINATION PISTONS
General Pistons   0   1   2
Toggle switch setter board

ACTION
Electro-pneumatic, Pitman type
Schwimmer winded

GRACE CHURCH ON-THE-HILL

300 Lonsdale Road
Casavant Organ Opus 1154, 1926, rebuilt 1961
Console rebuilt R.A. Denton 1997

Architect Eden Smith's design for Grace Church on-the-Hill was to have included a substantial tower at its east entrance. This was never built, but a stone belfry with a conical roof was added in 1938.

(Overleaf) The organ at Grace Church on the Hill is well placed to speak evenly to both the choir and congregation.

Grace Church on-the-Hill is the continuation of a parish which was first established in downtown Toronto on Elm Street between Elizabeth and Bay Streets in 1874. The parish was considered to offer an alternative to the "ritualistic practices" which were followed at the Church of the Holy Trinity, the second Anglican church in the neighborhood.

About that time an organ, Opus 33, was built by Edward Lye for "Grace Episcopal Church." It is probably safe to assume that it was for the Elm Street church.

A decision was taken in 1911 to move the parish to Forest Hill, at the time known as the "Hill District" or "College Heights," because it was found that over the years its downtown neighborhood was becoming less residential and many members, out of loyalty, were traveling great distances south to worship.

Property was purchased on Lonsdale Road just west of Russell Hill Road. The vendor indicated that if the church would consent to placing candles on its altar he would donate the land, but this offer was not accepted. Architect Eden Smith, who also designed St. Thomas's Church and St. John's Church, Portland Street, known as the Garrison Church, was retained to prepare designs for both a church and rectory.

The first phase of the church was constructed between 1912 and 1913. The church provided seating for 600 worshippers. In 1938 an addition was constructed, increasing seating, not counting the choir, to 800. This represented the completion of the Smith design except

for a tower which was to be 8.5 metres (28 feet) square and rise 29 metres (96 feet) at the main entrance. This tower was never built.

Grace Church on-the-Hill is constructed of Credit Valley limestone with Indiana limestone trim. This trim detail carries into the interior, where the walls have an off-white plaster finish. There is a medieval quality about the architecture, and Smith has tried to capture some of the simplicity of a Celtic abbey church or an early English parish church. The Arts and Crafts movement, of which Smith was a part, venerated medieval craftsmanship. The chancel is particularly spacious. The east windows, placed high above an elaborate stone reredos, are a trademark of the medieval period.

The present organ was built in 1926 and was a gift of the Honourable R. C. Matthews in memory of his daughter, Helen Matthews Somerville.

For many years the organ was the examination organ for the Canadian College of Organists. A chart showing the stops and couplers was printed in the CCO Yearbook. In 1961, during the tenure of organist John M. Hodgins, the organ was tonally revised in the style of the day. All of the stops on the Great were new, open-toe, un-nicked pipes. New mixtures and upper work were made for the Swell, Choir and Pedal.

In 1997 Grace Church On-the-Hill took steps to improve the nave and renovate the chancel area of the church. A hardwood floor was installed throughout the church. Following liturgical trends, a new altar was placed at the chancel steps, with the stone high altar remaining, and the choir stalls were replaced with movable risers and pews to provide for more flexible use of the space for a variety of performances. It was to facilitate this project that the organ console was converted to solid-state and placed on a rolling platform.

Casavant Organ Opus 1154, 1926, rebuilt 1961
Console rebuilt R.A. Denton 1997

GREAT ORGAN		FEET	PIPES
1	Quintaton	16	56
2	Diapason	8	56
3	Bourdon	8	56
4	Erzahler	8	56
5	Octave	4	56
6	Koppel Flote	4	56
7	Twelfth	2-2/3	56
8	Fifteenth	2	56
9	Fourniture IV	1-1/3	224
10	Scharf III	2/3	168
11	Trompette Harmonique (from # 34)	8	—

SWELL ORGAN (ENCLOSED)			
12	Geigen Principal	8	56
13	Stopped Diapason	8	56
14	Viola da Gamba	8	56
15	Voix Celeste Ten C	8	44
16	Geigen Octave	4	56
17	Klein Flote	4	56
18	Nazard	2-2/3	56
19	Octavin	2	56
20	Tertian II	1-3/5	112
21	Plein Jeu IV	1	224
22	Fagotto	16	56
23	Trompette	8	56
24	Oboe	8	56
25	Clarion	4	56
	Tremulant		

CHOIR ORGAN (ENCLOSED)			
26	Rohrflote	8	56
27	Gemshorn	8	56
28	Spitzprincipal	4	56
29	Dolce Flute	4	56
30	Italian Principal	2	56
31	Quinte	1-1/3	56
32	Sifflote	1	56
33	Clarinet	8	56
	Tremulant		

34	Trompette Harmonique	8	56

PEDAL ORGAN			
35	Resultant (12 quint pipes)	32	12
36	Contrabass	16	30
37	Bourdon	16	30
38	Quintaton (from #1)	16	—
39	Principal	8	30
40	Stopped Diapason (ext # 37)	8	12
41	Dolce	8	30
42	Choralbass	4	30
43	Fourniture IV	2-2/3	120
44	Trombone	16	30
45	Fagotto (from # 22)	16	—

COUPLERS
Great, Swell, Choir to Pedal 8, 4
Swell, Choir to Great 16, 8, 4
Swell to Choir 16, 8, 4
Great to Great 4, 8 off
Swell to Swell 16, 8 off, 4
Choir to Choir 16, 8 off, 4
Great to Choir

ADJUSTABLE COMBINATION PISTONS (electronic, 32 levels)
Great   1 2 3 4 5 6   Thumb
Swell   1 2 3 4 5 6   Thumb
Choir   1 2 3 4 5 6   Thumb
Pedal   1 2 3 4 5 6   Thumb
                              & Toe
General 1 2 3 4 5 6 7 8
                              Thumb & Toe
Adjuster
General Cancel
Pedal and Great Combination
Great Choir transfer

REVERSIBLES
Great, Swell, Choir to Pedal
Pedal Resultant 32 Thumb
Full Organ Thumb & Toe

ACTION
Electro pneumatic,
    Ventil stop action
The chests were originally of 68-note compass

23

CHURCH OF THE HOLY FAMILY

1372 King Street West
Gabriel Kney Organ built about 1980 for the Residence of Mr. Gordon Jeffery
Moved and revised in 2001 by Gober Organs Inc.

Holy Family R. C. Church. The Gabriel Kney Organ revised and re-installed by Halbert Gober. The main case is new and was built to match the existing Rückpositiv case.

A cupola, clad in copper is hardly perceptible through the trees, but through its circular windows daylight bathes the altar below.

On June 13, 1997, the Parkdale neighborhood of Toronto was saddened by the loss to fire of one of the local landmarks, the 1902 Church of the Holy Family. With the church went its 2-manual, 20-stop, mechanical action organ, Opus 27, built by Gerhard Brunzema ten years earlier.

Parkdale had emerged as a popular lakeside community in the 1870s, and with the growth of the incorporated village's population there was a flurry of church organization and building. An 1880 survey showed that 86 percent of Parkdale's 820 residents were equally distributed among the Anglican, Methodist and Presbyterian denominations. Each soon embarked on the construction of a house of worship of some size and architectural stature. The same survey indicated that fewer than 50 residents were Roman Catholic.

The construction of the first Church of the Holy Family began, therefore, relatively late, and the building designed by architect Arthur W. Holmes in a Gothic Revival style was not imposing. John Ross Robertson, in his *Landmarks of Toronto,* noted that the congregation "is neither wealthy nor especially influential, but they contribute most liberally of their means."

Catherine Palmer, for over 25 years the Director of Music of Yorkminster Park Baptist Church, once noted that, while the make-up of congregations change with the passage of time and the passing of personalities, the basic character of a congregation would seem to remain consistent.

When faced with the need to replace its destroyed church, the Parish of the Holy Family, under the leadership and spiritual guidance of the Fathers of the Oratory, successfully secured the required funds and built a new church which greatly surpassed the building that it had lost. Based on a per-square-foot cost, the new church is reputed to be the most costly Roman Catholic church built in Toronto during the past half century.

The Congregation of the Oratory was convinced that the new church should be built in a Renaissance or Classical Revival style. The Order's origins date back to St. Philip Nervi who lived in Italy during the Renaissance. Other important Oratorian centers, such as the Brompton Oratory in London and the Birmingham Oratory built in the latter half of the 19th century, had been constructed in the English Renaissance style which was a revival of the English Baroque of the 17th century. The Oratorians place a strong emphasis on art and music.

The Church of the Holy Family, designed by architect Brian T. E. Atkins of Thornhill, was dedicated in early 2001. It is a salmon-brick building with pre-cast concrete trim around doors and windows. The church is laid out in a traditional cruciform plan, with the Blessed Sacrament placed in an apse located behind, and to the north of, the main altar. The nave is proportionally tall and features a cupola centered over a marble altar set on a marble podium of stunning beauty. Other decorative items include a contemporary but elaborate wrought-iron gate screening the Blessed Sacrament, and the classically detailed organ case on the rear gallery. Amber glass clerestory windows bring golden light onto cream-coloured plaster walls and the ceramic tiled floor. The walls are intended to be adorned, in time, with religious imagery.

Gordon D. Jeffery, BA, FRCCO (HON) studied organ with Dr. Charles Peaker, Dr. Healey Willan and Ernest White. He was Registrar of the CCO from 1942 and then President of the RCCO from 1955 to 1957. His considerable wealth was derived from his profession as a lawyer and the family connection with the London Life Insurance Company.

Few of Gordon Jeffery's associates in the organ field knew of his skill as a skater. In 1953 he went to Oslo, Norway, as Canadian judge for the World Championship figure skating contests. On the same trip, he gave six concerts as organist and conductor.

In his lifetime his accomplishments as a patron of the arts included the conversion of a church into Aeolian Hall, London, Ontario, installation there of the Aeolian-Skinner Organ from St. Mary the Virgin, New York, the purchase of the old London Town Hall after the first Aeolian Hall burned in 1968, and the installation of a Gabriel Kney organ in the second hall. The

organ given to Holy Family Church by the estate of Gordon Jeffery was yet another organ, one which he had built for a large music room attached to his home in London, Ontario.

Most of the stops in the organ were rescaled by Halbert Gober as the pipes were built with small scales more suitable for a house organ. All ranks were revoiced for the new acoustic and a new façade was built to match the original Rückpositiv façade.

The Choir Organ is a floating division on an electric slider chest. Pedal pipes and chests for 4 stops were from an Ernest White Studio organ. Ernest White was a native of London, Ontario. He studied with Willan and MacMillan and then, in 1927, with Lynnwood Farnam in New York. He was organist and music director at St. Mary the Virgin, New York City for 25 years. He also became a tonal director for M. P. Moller Inc.

Gabriel Kney Organ built about 1980 for the Residence of Mr. Gordon Jeffery Moved and revised in 2001 by Gober Organs Inc.

Great Organ

		FEET	PIPES
1*	Bourdon	16	58
2	Praestant	8	58
3	Rohrflöte	8	58
4	Octav	4	58
5	Offenflöte	4	58
6	Quinteflöte	2-2/3	58
7	Octav	2	58
8	Terz	1-3/5	58
9	Mixture IV	1-1/3	232
10	Zimbel II	1/2	116
11	Trompete (1-12 H/L)	8	58
	3 spare stop buttons		

Swell Organ (enclosed)

		FEET	PIPES
12*	Bourdon (from #1)	16	—
13*	Bourdon (from #1)	8	—
14	Flûte (harmonic from 34)	8	58
15	Gamba (1-16 Haskells)	8	58
16	Céleste (from A 22)	8	37
17	Prinzipal	4	58
18	Flûte (harmonic from 20)	4	58
19	Nasat	2-2/3	58
20	Octavin	2	58
21	Tierce	1-3/5	58
22	Plein jeu V	2	290
23	Basson (1-12 H/L)	16	58
24	Trompette	8	58
25	Hautbois	8	58
26	Voix Humaine	8	58
27	Clairon	4	58
	Tremulant		
	3 spare stop buttons		

Ruckpositiv

		FEET	PIPES
28	Gedackt	8	58
29	Praestant	4	58
30	Octav	2	58
31	Blockflöte	1	58
32	Scharff III	1	174
	Tremulant		

Choir Organ (enclosed)

		FEET	PIPES
33*	Bourdon (from #1)	16	—
34*	Bourdon (from #1)	8	—
35*	Offenflöte	8	58
36*	Salizional (1-12 Haskells)	8	58
37*	Celeste Ten C	8	46
38*	Offenflöte	4	58
39*	Quint	2-2/3	58
40*	Blockflöte	2	58
41*	Terz	1-3/5	58
42*	Krummhorn	8	58
	Ventil		
	Tremulant		
	6 spare stop buttons		

Pedal Organ

		FEET	PIPES
43*	Subbass (1-8 from #1)	16	24
44*	Bourdon (from #1)	16	—
45*	Bassflöte (ext # 43)	8	12
46	Prinzipal (1-6 from #2)	8	26
47	Quint	5-1/3	32
48	Choralbass	4	32
49*	Mixture III	2-2/3	96
50*	Cornet III	3-1/5	96
51*	Posaune	16	32
	12 spare stop buttons		

Couplers

Great, Swell, Pos., Choir to Pedal
Swell, Pos., Choir to Great
Choir to Swell, Swell to Positiv

Combination Pistons
(SSL electronic 8 levels)

Great	1 2 3 4 5 6	Thumb
Swell	1 2 3 4 5 6	Thumb
Pos / Ch	1 2 3 4 5 6	Thumb
Pedal	1 2 3 4 5 6	Toe
General	1 2 3 4 5 6	Thumb & Toe
	7 8 9 10 11 12	Thumb

General Cancel
Adjuster
6 manual reversibles, 6 pedal reversibles

Full Organ thumb and toe reversible

Swell and Choir expression
Crescendo Pedal programmable 3 modes

Analysis

	STOPS	RANKS	PIPES	REAL STOPS
Great	11	15	864	11
Swell	16	18	1023	14
Positiv	5	7	406	5
Choir	10	8	452	8
Pedal	9	11	350	7
Totals	51	59	3095	45

Action
Mechanical key action and electric stop action except Pedal and stops marked *. Wind pressure 80 mm. Pedal 90 mm.

ISLINGTON UNITED CHURCH

25 Burnhamthorpe Road
Schoenstein & Co. 1993 San Francisco, California

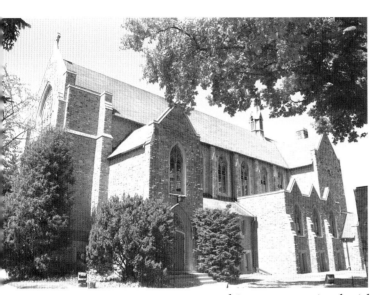

The organ chambers of Islington United Church are representative of an architectural anomaly which has challenged both acousticians and organ builders. An instrument and those who wish to appreciate it should be in the same room.

The Modern Gothic design of Islington United Church was found to have been so successful, that the Church of St. Timothy was inspired to build its twin in North Toronto.

Before there were populations to support a local Methodist church or even a minister, many communities which now make up Metropolitan Toronto were serviced by the Methodist Circuit Rider. It was the Circuit Rider from Adelaide Methodist Church, the forerunner of Metropolitan United Church, who included the community which was later to become Islington on his circuit. In 1843 it was finally possible to build a first church, Wesley Methodist Church, and in 1887 a second one, Islington Methodist Church, located on Dundas Road in the town of Islington.

The building which today we know as Islington United Church was first discussed in 1925. By 1936 an architect was retained with the intent of commencing construction by 1940, but World War II intervened and the idea was not taken up again until 1945, by the minister of the congregation, the Rev. John Coulter.

Construction began in 1947 and was completed in 1949. Islington United could well be the latest of the Modern Gothic churches built in this city. The architect was Bruce, Brown and Brisley. St. Timothy's, North Toronto, used the same design a year or two later.

Stone masons were brought from Scotland to raise the Credit Valley stone walls to a height of 20 metres (66 feet) above the street, the height of the chancel gable. Cornerstones of the two preceding church buildings were set into the walls of the entranceway; however, on the instructions of the Board of Trustees, the cornerstone from the 1843 church was soon removed. It was felt by some that, because this second church had been sold to the township and had been used for dances, political meetings and other worldly activities, it was not fitting to have its cornerstone included in the new edifice.

The plan of the church is that of a Latin cross, a traditional plan which has been followed by many cathedrals. The transepts of Islington United Church were not constructed until 1954, the same year that the portion of the building known as "Church House" was added, and, to complete the building's Gothic silhouette, the fleche over the chancel area.

In 1949 the Women's Association purchased a three-manual Casavant Organ, Opus 512, built in 1913 for West End Presbyterian Church. It was originally a tubular pneumatic organ and was electrified and combined with a console, Casavant Opus 811, 1919 from Knox Presbyterian Church in St. Catharines. In 1963

plans were prepared for a new Casavant organ. There was to be a Great and Positif Organ cantilevered into the chancel and Swell and Pedal in the loft. The new three-manual console was built in 1963 and the Positif Organ in 1976. The organ then had a total of 2,350 pipes. In 1993 the organ was sold to St. Andrew's United Church in Peterborough.

A new two-manual organ was built by Schoenstein in 1993 incorporating the Pedal Open Wood 16′ and Bourdon 16′ pipes. The entire organ is in the organ chamber and enclosed with double enclosure for the Solo pipes reminiscent of the Morel Organ of 1928 in St. James-Bond United Church.

Schoenstein & Co. 1993
San Francisco, California

GREAT ORGAN (ENCLOSED)

1	Contra Gamba	16	61
2	Open Diapason	8	61
3	Harmonic Flute	8	61
4	Gamba (ext # 1)	8	12
5*	Lieblich Gedackt	8	61
6	Principal	4	61
7	Lieblich Gedackt (ext #5)	4	12
8	Fifteenth	2	61
9	Mixture IV	1-1/3	244
10	Corno di bassetto (ext #11)	16	12
11	Corno di bassetto	8	61
12	Tuba (Solo)	8	—
	Harp (Swell)		
	Chimes (Swell)		
	Tremulant		
	Great Octave		

SWELL ORGAN (ENCLOSED)

13	Bourdon (ext #15)	16	12
14	Open Diapason	8	61
15	Stopped Diapason	8	61
16	Echo Gamba	8	61
17	Vox Angelica	8	61
18	Gemshorn (12 from #15)	8	49
19	Octave (ext #14)	4	12
20	Flute	4	61
21	Chimney Flute	4	61
22	Nazard (from # 21)	2-2/3	—
23	Piccolo (ext # 21)	2	12
24	Tierce Ten C	1-3/5	49
25	Mixture III-IV	2	na
26	Posaune	16	61
27	Trumpet	8	61
28	Hautboy	8	61
29	Vox Humana** (in Solo box)	8	61
30	Clarion (ext # 27)	4	12
	Harp (electronic in Solo box) 61 generators		
	Chimes Ten C (electronic in Solo box) 32 generators		
	Tremulant		
	Swell Sub, Super, 8 off		

SOLO ORGAN
(ENCLOSED SEPARATELY WITHIN SWELL BOX, PLAYABLE FROM SWELL)

31	Double Tuba Ten C (from# 32)	16	—
32	Tuba (15"wind, hooded)	8	61
33	Tuba Clarion (ext #32)	4	12

PEDAL ORGAN

34	Resultant (wired)	32	—
35*	Open Wood (enclosed)	16	32
36*	Sub Bass (enclosed)	16	32
37	Contra Gamba (from #1)	16	—
38	Open Diapason (from #2)	8	—
39	Flute (from #5)	8	—
40	Contra Posaune (in Swell box, electronic, 32 generators)	32	—
41	Ophicleide (in Swell box)	16	32
42	Posaune (from # 26)	16	—
43	Corno di bassetto (from #10)	16	—
44	Octave Posaune (from #26)	8	—
45	Corno di bassetto (from #11)	4	—

*   Pipes from former organ
** With separate tremolo and adjustable enclosure

COUPLERS

Great to Pedal
     (Super Octave reading
     through)
Swell to Pedal
     (Super Octave reading
     through)
Swell to Great
     (Octaves reading through)
Great to Swell
Solo and Percussion unaffected
     by couplers

Adjustable Combination Pistons
     (solid state, 16 memories)
     33 pistons and toe studs
     5 reversibles

ANALYSIS

	STOPS	RANKS	PIPES	REAL STOPS
Great	12	11	707	8
Swell	18	16	983	13
Solo	3	1	73	1
Pedal	13	3	96	3
Totals	46	31	1859	24

ACTION
Electric pneumatic, unit type

30

JARVIS STREET BAPTIST CHURCH

130 Gerrard Street East
Karn-Warren, 1912, rebuilt 1987-1991 by Andrew Mead
Casavant console 1989

The corner of Jarvis Street at Gerrard was the new home of a Baptist congregation whose previous home had been on Bond Street. The new Jarvis Street Baptist Church was built in 1874-75 to a design by the firm of Langley, Langley & Burke. Its Decorated Gothic Revival style was considered to be *de rigueur* for ecclesiastical architecture in the 1870s. It does not, however, follow the usual basilican plan but boasts the first amphitheatrical church interior in Canada. Strongly stated brownstone walls, contrasted with a wealth of fluid detailing, frame a riveting tower and spire placed diagonally at the main intersection.

The construction of Jarvis Street Baptist Church was one of several projects guided to completion by the businessman and philanthropist William McMaster. Others included McMaster College, today the Royal Conservatory of Music, also designed by Langley, and the Toronto Necropolis.

Pastor Thomas Todhunter Shields led the congregation of Jarvis Street Baptist Church for forty years, filling its central pulpit with powerful oratory. "He used his voice like a musician using the stops of an organ…" were the words that one Toronto newspaperman used to describe the Reverend Shields.

A two-manual organ designed by William Horatio Clarke was installed in the new building, incorporating some Clarke inventions. Blown by a water motor, the organ had a Great of 15 stops and a Swell of 15 stops. At some point between 1878 and 1900, the Jarvis Street organ was converted to three manuals and electric action. And again in 1936, a new three-manual console was built by Cyril and Harold Robbins for Jarvis Street.

The church was gutted by fire in 1936, but was immediately rebuilt in accordance with the existing plan. During the restoration by Horwood & White, Langley's successor firm, the west doors and flanking gargoyles were added. Inside, the rebuilt room is washed in golden light, from windows and from an impressive "rose window" of amber glass placed centrally in the ceiling of the room and filtering natural light from the skylights above.

In 1939, Jarvis Street Baptist purchased and installed a Karn-Warren organ from

Few people would guess that the twin entrance porches, in the west facade of Jarvis Street Baptist Church are not original. They were added, along with the flanking gargoyles, after the building was gutted by fire in 1936.

First St. Andrew's United Church in London, Ontario. This organ had originally been built in 1893 by C. S. Warren for the Presbyterian Church in London, and was rebuilt in 1912 by Karn Warren for the new church which became First St. Andrew's United. It was this 1912 organ which was installed in the Jarvis Street Church.

The organ case was designed by Horwood and White, Architects, and built by the Globe Furniture Company. The gilt pipes framed in the delicately detailed woodwork of the organ case provide a fitting backdrop to the pulpit, choir loft and baptistry *en fenêtre*.

The organ was rebuilt yet again in 1985. Andrew Mead, church member and employee of Alan T. Jackson & Company, began rebuilding the organ and incorporated the 1937 swell and great Pitman chests from the Casavant organ of St. John's Anglican Church, Pembroke, Bermuda; a 1928 Casavant Ventil chest converted to Pitman for the Choir; original Karn-Warren reservoirs and offset chests (restored); and a new 32', half length pedal reed from P & S of Suffolk, England. The project was completed in 1991.

The organ case at Jarvis Street Baptist Church was designed by Horwood and White, Architects and built by the Globe Furniture Company. The handsome effect is due in part to the use of pipe shades so that none of the tops of the pipes in the façade are allowed to show.

The new Casavant console has drawstops and key sharps of rosewood and manual key coverings of bone.

Karn-Warren, 1912, rebuilt 1987-1991 by Andrew Mead Casavant console 1989

Great Organ		Feet	Pipes
1	Double Open Diapason	16	61
2	Open Diapason	8	61
3	Doppel Flute	8	61
4	Chimney Flute	8	61
5	Principal	4	61
6	Harmonic Flute	4	61
7	Twelfth	2-2/3	61
8	Fifteenth	2	61
9	Tierce	1-3/5	61
10	Mixture	IV	244
11	Trumpet	8	61
	Great 4 Coupler		

Swell Organ (enclosed)			
12	Open Diapason	8	61
13	Stopped Flute	8	61
14	Gamba	8	61
15	Céleste Ten C	8	49
16	Principal	4	61
17	Wald Flute	4	61
18	Flageolet	2	61
19	Mixture	III	183
20	Bassoon (prepared)	16	—
21	Trompette	8	61
22	Oboe	8	61
	Tremulant		
	Swell 16, 4 Couplers		

Choir Organ (enclosed)			
23	Rohr Flute	8	61
24	Principal	4	61
25	Cornet II	2-2/3	122
26	Flute	2	61
27	Mixture	III	183
28	Clarinet	8	61
	Tremulant		
	Chimes (prepared)		

Pedal Organ			
29	Open Diapason (wood)	16	32
30	Open Diapason (metal)	16	32
31	Bourdon	16	32
32	Octave	8	32
33	Flute (ext #31)	8	12
34	Super Octave (ext #32)	4	12
35	Double Trombone H/L	32	12
36	Trombone	16	32
37	Bassoon (prepared)	16	—

Couplers
Great, Swell, Choir to Pedal
Great 4 to Pedal
Swell to Great 16, 8, 4
Choir to Great 8, 4
Swell to Choir 16, 8, 4

Combination Pistons
SSL electronic 8 levels of memory

KNOX COLLEGE CHAPEL

University of Toronto, 59 St. George Street
Hellmuth Wolff & Associés Ltée
Opus 33, 1991, Gallery

The stop list of the Knox College organ follows very closely that of the 1726 Cahman instrument in the Leufsta, Bruk, Sweden. The case design, however, is similar only in colour. The Toronto organ is of angular, Gothic form and the Swedish organ is Baroque. Spread across a wide gallery are three organ cases, festooned with curved decorations and carved figures.

In 1912, not long after the completion of construction of their design for Rosedale Presbyterian Church, the architects Chapman & McGiffin won a competition for the design of Knox College on the campus of the University of Toronto. This was at a time when churches, schools and colleges were beginning to be designed in a robust and often simplified reinstatement of the Gothic form. The idiom became known as Modern Gothic or Collegiate Gothic. Havergal College on Avenue Road, was also designed by Chapman & McGiffin in this style. Patricia McHugh, in her book *Toronto Architecture*, suggests that it was a style which offered the reassurance of "pastness" at the beginning of a new century that was characterized by rapid and confusing change.

Knox College is a building of Norman inspiration. A description provided in the January/February 1925 issue of the *Journal of the Royal Architectural Institute of Canada* was particularly complimentary with respect to the clarity of the college's design. "Knox College is a worthy addition to the group of buildings surrounding the main campus.... The story of its requirements is told in a very simple, yet distinguished and artistic manner. Any casual observer looking at the eastern or principal façade... cannot fail to see the chapel on the south, the oriel window to the north, meaning two floors, with a library above and classrooms below. The names of Knox and Calvin on the escutcheons must lead to the conclusion that this is a Presbyterian theological college and

At the time when Knox College moved to its new Modern Gothic building of Norman inspiration, the College had been in existence for close to seventy years.

that the students should feel happy that they have such a beautiful building in which to labour."

The chapel has a simplicity, even a starkness, which contributes both to its success as a place of worship and to its acoustic. The walls are made of dressed stone and are articulated by a line of widely spaced columns along the inside edge of the side aisles. Some warmth is contributed by the oak fittings and the carved trusses which support the roof. Amber-coloured glass is set in large traceried window openings, and during the day the room is infused with a golden hue. There are shallow transepts, and, in the westerly transept, there is a balcony.

When the Hellmut Wolff organ was commissioned in the late 1980s, a decision was made to place the new instrument on a new gallery at the rear of the chapel. This gallery was designed by architect Denis Lamarre in consultation with the organ builder. While structurally it is a concrete slab on steel beams, these have been covered with oak and complement the case of the organ in detail and in colour, which is two shades of green. The organ case has been designed to sympathize with the Gothic detailing of the room, rather than to reflect the Baroque inspiration of the organ.

Hauptwerk, Pedal and Positiv pipes are constructed and scaled after Johan Niclas Cahmen's organ in Leufsta Bruk, Sweden. The scales of the pipes in the Brustwerk follow Huss and Schnittger. The organ is tuned according to a modified mean-tone tuning devised by Herwin Troje following 17th century Swedish theorists.

The key action is suspended and self-regulating. The stop action is also mechanical with three reversible pedals for Hauptwerk and Pedal reeds. Two cuneiform bellows deliver the wind. These bellows operate in sequence and may be pumped either by foot or fed by an electric blower. The builder has made this statement about the winding:

> The wind at Knox is quite lively. There is not much difference between hand-blown and motor-blown wind, but one can notice the hand-blown wind responds better to repeated chords and runs in the left hand when there are sustained notes in the treble. The reason is quite obvious: when hand-blown the bass of the bellows moves only downwards, when operated by blower, the bellows may have to reverse their movement quickly, which can perturb the wind.

The Casavant chancel organ, Opus 624, 1915 is divided into two chambers at the front of the chapel. It was built with three manuals, 26 stops and 24 ranks of pipes. The action is electro-pneumatic with Ventil chests. In 1959 a new console was built and in 1974, a Mixture IV was added to the Great Organ. There were two special instructions to the builder in the original contract. One was that the blower motor run on direct current, and the other that the Great Trumpet 8' be "smoothly voiced."

Hellmuth Wolff & Associés Ltée
Opus 33, 1991, Gallery

HAUPTWERK C-F'''
(HUFWUDWERKET) 54 NOTES

1	Qwintadena	16
2	Principal	8
3	Ror-Fleut	8
4	Octawa	4
5	Spets-Fleut	4
6	Qwinta	2-2/3
7	Superoctawa	2
8	Mixtur III orV	1-1/3
9	Trumpet	8

POSITIV C-F'''
(RYGG-POSITIVT) 54 NOTES

10	Gedagt	8
11	Qwintadena	8
12	Principal	4
13	Gedagt-Fleut	4
14	Sexquuialtra	II
15	Quinta	2-2/3
16	Octawa	2
17	Mixtur II or IV	1-1/3
18	Dulcian	8

Brustwerk C,D,E,F,G,A–d'''
(Brostwerket) 47 notes

19	Gedagt	8
20	Fleut	4
21	Wald-Fleut	2
22	Tertian	II
23	Qwinta	1-1/3
24	Regal	8

Pedal C–f' 30 notes

25	Subb-Bass	16
26	Principal	8
27	Gedagt	8
28	Octawa	4
29	Mixtur V	2-2/3
30	Basun	16
31	Trumpet	8
32	Cornett	2

Fogelsang
Tremulant

Couplers
Positiv / Pedal
Hauptwerk / Pedal
Positiv / Hauptwerk
(shove coupler)

Mixture Composition
Hauptwerk Mixture III or IV
    5 ranks: after Cahman
    3 ranks : tierces cancelled
    (half draw)

C	G#	c'	f#'	c''
(1-1/3)	1-1/3 (2-2/3)	2-2/3 (5-1/3)		
1	1	2	2	4
(4/5)	(4/5)	(1-3/5)	(1-3/5)	(3-1/5)
2/3	2/3	1-1/3	1-1/3	2-2/3
1/2	(1/2)	1	(1)	2

Positiv Mixtur II or IV
    4 ranks: after Cahman
    2 ranks: tierces cancelled
    (half draw)

C	f#	f#'	c''	f#''
(1-1/3)	1-1/3 (2-2/3)	2-2/3 (5-1/3)		
1	1	2	2	4
(4/5)	(4/5)	(1-3/5)	(1-3/5)	(3-1/5)
2/3	(2/3)	1-1/3	(1-1/3)	2-2/3

Pedal Mixtur V (without breaks)

2-2/3	2	1-3/5	1-1/3	1

The casework of the Casavant Organ in Lawrence Park Community Church displays the lowest notes of the principals of the Grand Orgue and Pédale.

LAWRENCE PARK COMMUNITY CHURCH

2180 Bayview Avenue
Casavant Organ Opus 3768, 1998

When the Lawrence Park Community was conceived by Wilfred Servington Dinnick, the young English-born president of the Standard Loan Co., and designed by the English consulting engineer W.S. Brooke in 1907-08, it was envisioned as a strictly residential enclave for the "comfortably off" or "well-to-do," with no provision for schools, churches or shops. Lawrence Park was the Canadian sequel to the development of the garden city in England, the first being Letchworth in 1902.

Some 35 years later a group of thoughtful members of the community realized that they should have a church where they and their neighbors could worship. Services began in the auditorium of Blythwood School in December 1945. It was unusual that this group was composed of representatives of all the mainline Protestant denominations, together with members of the Jewish, Quaker and Roman Catholic faiths. While initially the consensus was that the new church remain non-denominational, the difficulty of finding ministers not denominationally ordained moved the congregation to seek affiliation with The United Church of Canada.

A site was found on the easterly edge of the community at the southwest corner of St. Leonard's and Bayview Avenues – property originally described as "wet ground." This land was purchased in 1947 from Mrs. E. R. Wood, widow of the founder of Dominion Securities and owner of Glendon Hall. The site was drained to the nearby ravine under Bayview Avenue.

With Gordon Adamson and Associates selected as the architect, development of the facility proceeded over three phases. Initially the central part of the building, comprising main floor offices and a second floor auditorium, was constructed, opening for use in

time, an organ chamber was added to the west end of the 1952 chancel in order to accommodate the church's first pipe organ.

Following World War II, church architecture quickly abandoned its nostalgia for Victorian precedents. There are likely many reasons for this change of direction.

May 1949. Subsequently the nave of the church, the narthex and the chancel were built, with the first service of worship in the sanctuary held on September 14, 1952. The third unit, the Christian Education Building, was completed three years later. At about the same

Without being conclusive, we point to but a few.

The returning Canadian troops came home not only with the experience of having seen some of the great ecclesiastical architecture, but also with a world view. During the interwar years, western Europe had been experiencing the impact of the German Bauhaus. Many architects were pioneering Modernism, with its desire to simplify and eliminate the superfluous. The rebuilding of Coventry Cathedral in the early 1950s by Sir Basil Spence, not in a style reminiscent of the 15th century Gothic original but in a totally contemporary vocabulary, became a new benchmark for architects around the world.

In addition, the architectural detailing required by the revival styles pushed the cost of building in these forms beyond the means of many congregations. A range of alternatives appeared. Most usual was the "A-frame." In this form the ridge remained high, maintaining visibility and verticality, but the overall volume requiring heating was reduced. Compared to the cost of masonry, the cost of roofing was relatively cheap, although, of course, re-roofing costs were never put into the equation. Examples of the A-frame include Humber Valley United Church and St. Monica's Anglican Church on Hiawatha Road. Another common form was the shoebox, often one simple rectangular space under a flat roof, with no articulation of nave and chancel; an example of this is the Church of the Comforter, today St. Luke's Church, on Coxwell Avenue.

The most unusual church built in Toronto in the 1950s was a replacement building for the Parish of St. Hilda's, Fairbank, built in 1954. St. Hilda's made use of two reinforced concrete hyperbolic shells. One shell formed the nave and a second the crossing, a structural form first used for airship hangers at Orly, near Paris (1916-24). It was a great sadness to see this monumental structure succumb to the wrecker's ball in 1995.

At one time the M. P. Moller Company was the largest builder of pipe organs in the world, with over 400 employees. Whatever conditions changed to bring

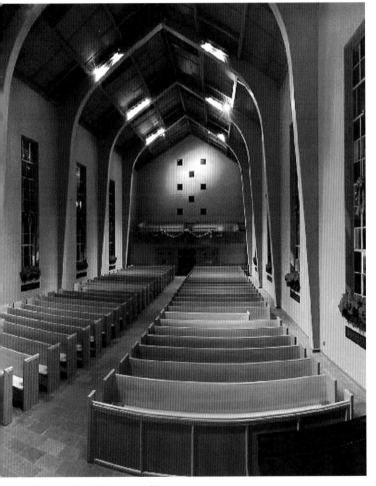

The use of multiplex control for organs has eliminated the problem of deciding where to install consoles. The Lawrence Park console can be rolled easily to any point on the tile platform.

about the closing of the firm in 1992, the question of serviceability would have had some bearing on the failure. The Moller Organ installed in 1956 at Lawrence Park had problems of placement, being crowded into four levels reaching the peak of the roof. It also suffered from the basic builders' error of running the key channels through the bottom boards of the windchests. In effect this meant that the bottom boards ran in the wrong direction so that a simple repair of a valve became a major repair. In order to remove the actions for one stop it was necessary to take down the bottom boards of the whole chest section.

Because the key channels were in the bottom boards, Moller was unable to take advantage of space-saving, economical schwimmer wind systems. The working space under the organ was a jumble of reservoirs and large wind lines.

The pedal and smaller windchests of the Lawrence Park Moller were retained for the new organ since they were of more standard construction and serviceable.

The donor of the 1956 organ was the family of the late Mr. J. S. McLean, first president of Canada Packers. The new organ was dedicated on October 18, 1998 and is named for the major donor, Florence Grand.

Casavant Organ Opus 3768, 1998

GRAND ORGUE		FEET	PIPES
1	Violon	16	61
2	Montre	8	61
3	Flûte à cheminée	8	61
4	Flûte harmonique (1-19 common with #3)	8	42
5	Prestant	4	61
6	Flûte ouverte	4	61
7	Doublette	2	61
8	Flûte	2	61
9	Cornet II	2-2/3	122
10	Fourniture IV-V	1-1/3	269
11	Trompette	8	61

Grand Orgue Unison Off

12	Trompette royale (Choeur)	8	—

Flûte Tremblant
Grand Orgue 4' Coupler
Chimes (A-e, 21 notes)
MIDI

RÉCIT (ENCLOSED)			
13*	Bourdon doux (1-12 ext #15)	16	12
14	Principal	8	61
15	Bourdon	8	61
16*	Viole de gambe	8	61
17*	Voix céleste	8	61
18	Octave	4	61
19*	Flûte douce	4	61
20	Octavin	2	61
21	Plein jeu IV	2	244
22	Basson (ext #23, 1-12 L/2)	16	12
23	Trompette	8	61
24	Hautbois	8	61
25	Voix humaine	8	61
26	Clairon	4	61

Récit 16, Unison Off, 4' Couplers
Tremblant

27	Trompette royale (Choeur)	8	—

MIDI

CHOEUR (ENCLOSED)			
28*	Cor de Chamois	8	61
29	Bourdon	8	61
30*	Erzahler	8	61
31*	Erzahler céleste (Ten C)	8	49
32	Prestant	4	61
33	Flûte à fuseau	4	61
34	Nazard	2-2/3	61
35	Quarte de nazard	2	61
36	Tierce	1-3/5	61
37	Larigot	1-1/3	61
38	Cymbale III	1	183
39	Clarinette	8	61

Choeur 16, Unison Off, 4' Couplers
Tremblant

40	Trompette royale (hooded)	8	61

MIDI

PÉDALE			
41	Basse résultante (from #42 & 44)	32	—
42*	Contrebasse (ext #46)	16	12
43*	Soubasse	16	32
44	Violon (from #1)	16	—
45	Bourdon doux (from #13)	16	—
46	Octavebasse	8	32
47*	Flûte bouchee (ext. #43)	8	12
48	Bourdon (from #15)	8	—
49	Octave	4	32
50*	Flûte (ext # 47)	4	12
51	Mixture II	2-2/3	64
52	Contre bombarde (half length, ext #53)	32	12
53	Bombarde (full length)	16	32
54	Contre trompette (from #22)	16	—
55	Trompette (ext #53)	8	12
56	Trompette royale (from #39)	8	—
57	Clairon (ext #55)	4	12

Chimes
MIDI

COUPLERS (IN TILTING TABLETS)

Grand Orgue, Récit, Choeur/ Pédale		8	4
Récit, Choeur/ Grand Orgue	16	8	4
Récit/Choeur	16	8	4

Grand Orgue/Choeur Reverse

ADJUSTABLE COMBINATIONS

(Capture system, electronic, 32 levels)

Grand orgue
  1 2 3 4 5 6 7 8   Thumb

Récit
  1 2 3 4 5 6 7 8   Thumb

Choeur
  1 2 3 4 5 6 7 8   Thumb

Pédale
  1 2 3 4 5 6 7 8   Thumb & Toe

METROPOLITAN UNITED CHURCH

56 Queen Street East
Casavant Organ, Opus 1367, Chancel Organ built 1930
Gallery Organ built 1998

General
1 2 3 4 5 6 7 8
9 10 11 12   Thumb &
                                     Toe
Cancel   Thumb
Adjuster(with lock)   Thumb

ANALYSIS   REAL

	STOPS	RANKS	PIPES	STOPS
Grand Orgue	12	16	921	11
Récit	15	15	939	12
Choeur	13	15	903	13
Pédale	17	6	264	5
Total	57	52	3027	41

REVERSIBLE PISTONS
Grand Orgue,
    Récit,
    Choeur/Pédale   Thumb & Toe
Récit, Choeur/
    Grand Orgue   Thumb
Récit/Choeur   Thumb
Résultante 32'   Toe
Contre bombarde 32'   Toe
Clochettes   Toe
Tutti   Thumb & Toe

Balanced Récit and Choeur
    expression pedals
Crescendo on all stops and
    couplers (programmable,
    4 modes)

ACTION
Electro-pneumatic, Pitman
    key and stop action

* pipes from Moller Organ

Metropolitan United Church's 104 foot high tower has the advantage of being viewed across a sizable front yard, which today is under the jurisdiction of the City of Toronto.

Although the Anglican St. James' Cathedral had served all denominations in York since 1805, by 1818 the Methodists of York felt a need for a chapel of their own. To that end, the Rev. Henry Ryan took out a mortgage on his farm located near Beamsville in order to purchase a property on King Street between Bay and Yonge Streets. A clapboard church measuring thirty by forty feet was constructed. By 1831 the population of the community had increased to 7,000 and a larger church was required to serve a congregation of 264. A two-storied church was opened in 1832 on the southeast corner of Toronto and Adelaide Streets.

By 1870, Toronto was becoming increasingly commercial and populated. Methodists had their own fair share of this new wealth and a number had been able to build homes in the upper Jarvis Street area which had become fashionable.

It was with the support of many of these families that a new property, bounded by Queen, Bond, Shuter and Church Streets, then known as McGill Square, was purchased. For a short while there was some public dissent around this sale, because although the land was privately held it had been in use as a public square. Parishioners of St. Michael's Roman Catholic Cathedral, for one, had always assumed that the Square would permit them to maintain an unencumbered view of the south elevation of their Cathedral.

Although a committee in charge of building the new

church had launched a competition for an appropriate design, the submissions were returned to their owners because they were too expensive for the available budget. The Committee then turned directly to Henry Langley, who had submitted a competition entry, for a new design and he promptly began work on the site.

The organ screens either side of the chancel at Metropolitan United Church have a powerful appearance suggestive of the power of the organ behind. In the east loft are the Great, Tuba and Pedal Organs. The Swell, Choir and Orchestral Organs are in three massive expression boxes in the west loft.

The interior of Metropolitan United Church is going through a metamorphosis visually and acoustically: sound absorbing, "acoustical" finishes are being removed in the course of a major redecorating, and the room is being returned to its former reverberant splendour.

Henry Langley was a likely candidate for the project. At the time, he was reported to be designing at least a dozen new churches, and in forty-four years of practice he designed over seventy churches and altered or renovated many more. At the time that he was retained by Metropolitan Methodist Church, he was just completing additions to St. Michael's Cathedral across the street.

Most of Langley's work is in the Gothic Revival style. Interestingly, earlier and later Methodist churches were distinguishable from buildings for Roman Catholics and Anglicans. They tended to be more influenced by Classical, Italianate and Romanesque influences. But in the 1860s and 1870s many Methodist and other Protestant churches leaned toward High Victorian Gothic.

From the exterior, Langley's design for Metropolitan Methodist Church resembled a 14th century French Gothic cathedral 66.5 metres (218 feet) long and 31.7 metres (104 feet) wide with a pinnacled tower at the main entrance, a long nave and a chancel at the north end. Inside, it was quite a different matter. They were still Methodists who worshipped in an auditorium. The auditorium was surrounded on three sides by a balcony supported on cast-iron columns. The seating capacity of the room was 1,800 which could be increased to 2,400 with temporary seating. What appeared to be a chancel on the exterior was known as the chapel and functioned as a meeting room, primarily for the assembly of the Sunday School. In 1925 Metropolitan Methodist became Metropolitan United Church.

On January 30, 1928 a fire came close to destroying the whole church. By the time the fire had been extinguished, the tower with its carillon, the narthex, the rear portion of the balcony, and the brick walls were all that could be saved. The church was reconstructed, but

43

with significant changes to its architecture.

What had previously appeared to be a chancel now actually became one, complete with a divided choir and organ chambers. The front of a new communion table, placed at the far end of the chancel, included a carving of the Last Supper after the painting by

The 1998 Gallery Organ of eight stops, seven ranks and 393 pipes employs twin cases of oak mounted on the rear wall of the gallery.

(Above, right) The Orchestral Trumpet in the Solo Organ, Metropolitan United Church employs 49 spun, brass trumpet resonators. The slender pipes beyond are the Viole d'Orchestre and the wooden pipes are the Gross Flute.

Leonardo da Vinci. Organ pipework is screened by richly carved oak woodwork which echoes Gothic design motifs. The stained glass windows were installed after the fire.

The Metropolitan United Church organ was a replacement to the Karn-Warren Organ of 1904. The great success of the Metropolitan United Church organ at the time of installation lay in its ability to cover a wide range of orchestral effects and to produce rapid crescendos and diminuendos from the extremely loud to the almost inaudible. Transcriptions of orchestral music were used as much as music for organ. Yet the

organ could interpret most organ repertoire – French, German and English – which meant that it survived the pressures for change from the Organ Reformers of the mid-twentieth century. Plans were drafted in 1976, in the time of organist Melville Cook, to build a new, low-pressure Great Organ at the head of the chancel. This was intended to help in the performance of classical organ music but also to give those seated toward the rear of the church some direct sound for listening and support for singing. These plans were never realized.

The arrival of the gallery organ in 1998 confirms this organ as the largest in Canada. More important, it made an immediate improvement in the congregational singing at the back of the church, surpassing expectations. It is one more confirmation of the old rule that the best place to build an organ is high on the central axis at the back or front of the room.

ORIGINS, REVISIONS, ADDITIONS

1872 O'Dell tracker organ

1875 S. R. Warren rebuilt the O'Dell Organ, the largest in Canada, 3 manuals, 3,315 pipes. The organ was later moved to Central United Church, Sault Ste. Marie, Ontario.

1904/1911 Karn Warren Organ of 93 ranks, a gift of Mrs. Lillian Massey Treble in memory of Hart A. Massey. It had a Great, Swell, Choir and Pedal at the front of the church and Tower Echo and Solo at the back (1904)

1928 Church and organ burned, January 30

1930 Casavant Organ Opus 1357 opened, 5 manuals, 121 ranks

1983 Remote, electro-pneumatic combination action replaced with Corlis solid-state system

1986 Remote, electro-pneumatic manual and pedal key contact relays and switches replaced with SSL system

1990 Flue pipes restored, coned pipes sleeved

1991 Reed pipes cleaned and restored.

1998 Gallery Organ of 8 stops, 2 divisions given by the Newcourt Credit Group in honour of Mr. Ronald A. McKinlay.

1998 Replaced Corlis combination action with new Artisan Classic system, 99 levels of memory.

Casavant Organ, Opus 1367, Chancel Organ built 1930 Gallery Organ built 1998

GREAT ORGAN		FEET	PIPES
1	Contra Bourdon (Ten C)	32	56
2	Double Open Diapason	16	68
3	Bourdon	16	68
4	Open Diapason I	8	68
5	Open Diapason II	8	68
6	Open Diapason III	8	68
7	Violin Diapason	8	68
8	Hohl Flute	8	68
9	Doppel Flute	8	68
10	Stopped Diapason	8	68
11	Quint	5-1/3	68
12	Octave	4	68
13	Principal	4	68
14	Flute Harmonique	4	68
15	Flute d'Amour	4	68
16	Twelfth	2-2/3	68
17	Fifteenth	2	61
18	Mixture 12, 15, 17 III		204
19	Harmonics 15,17, 19, b21, 22 V		340
20	Contra Tromba (h. press.)	16	68
21	Tromba (h. press.)	8	68
22	Posaune (h. press.)	8	68
23	Octave Tromba (h. press.)	4	68
	Harp (from Choir)		

SWELL ORGAN (ENCLOSED)			
24	Contra Geigen	16	68
25	Lieblich Bourdon	16	68
26	Open Diapason	8	68
27	Geigen Principal	8	68
28	Lieblich Gedeckt	8	68
29	Viola di Gamba	8	68
30	Salicional	8	68
31	Voix céleste	8	68
32	Aeoline	8	68
33	Octave	4	68
34	Flauto Traverso	4	68
35	Superoctave	2	61
36	Mixture 12, 15, 19, 22 III		204
37	Cornet 1, 8, 12, 15, 17 V		328
38	Double Trumpet (h.press.)	16	68
39	Trumpet (h. press.)	8	68
40	Oboe	8	68
41	Vox humana	8	68
42	Clarion (h.press.)	4	68
	Harp (from Choir)		
	Tremulant		

CHOIR ORGAN (ENCLOSED)			
43	Contra Viola	16	68
44	Open Diapason	8	68
45	Gamba	8	68
46	Melodia	8	68
47	Quintadena	8	68
48	Spitz Flute	8	68
49	Flute céleste	8	68
50	Dulciana	8	68
51	Unda Maris	8	68
52	Dulcet	4	68
53	Lieblich Flute	4	68
54	Nazard	2-2/3	68
55	Harmonic Piccolo	2	61
56	Tierce	1-3/5	61
57	Dulciana Mixture 12, 17, 19, 22 IV		272
58	Contra Fagotto	16	68
59	Clarinet	8	68
60	Trumpet	8	68
61	Clarion	4	68
62	Harp	61 bars	
	Harp Sub		
	Tremulant		

ORCHESTRAL ORGAN (ENCLOSED)			
63	Contra Gamba	16	68
64	Gross Gamba	8	68

(Continued overleaf)

65	Gamba céleste	8	68
66	Rohr Flute	8	68
67	Gross Flute	8	68
68	Viole d'Orchestre	8	68
69	Viole céleste II	8	136
70	Fugara	4	68
71	Concert Flute	4	68
72	Cornet de Violes 10, 12, 15 III		204
73	Bassoon	16	68
74	French Horn	8	68
75	Orchestral Oboe	8	68
76	Cor Anglais	8	68
77	Corno di Bassetto	8	68
78	Trombone	16	68
79	Orchestral Trumpet	8	68
80	Tuba Sonora	8	68
81	Octave tuba	4	68
	Harp (from Choir)		
	Tremulant		

BOMBARDE ORGAN

82	Stentorphone	8	61
83	Mixture 1, 5, 8, 12, 15, 19, 22 VII		427
84	Tuba Magna	16	61
85	Tuba Mirabilis	8	61
86	Quint Horn	5-1/3	61
87	Tuba Clarion	4	61

PEDAL ORGAN

88	Double Open Diapason	32	32
89	Open Diapason No.116		32
90	Open Diapason No.2 (ext #88)	16	12
91	Violone	16	32
92	Gamba (from #63)	16	—
93	Bourdon No 1	16	32
94	Bourdon No 2 (from #3)	16	—
95	Viola (from #43)	16	—
96	Gedeckt (from #25)	16	—
97	Quinte	10-2/3	32
98	Octave (ext #89)	8	12
99	Cello (ext #91)	8	12
100	Stopped Flute (ext #93)	8	12

101	Still Gedeckt (from #25)	8	—
102	Octave Quint (ext # 97)	5-1/3	12
103	Superoctave (ext #98)	4	12
104	Mixture 15,17,19,22 IV		128
105	Contra Bombarde	32	32
106	Bombarde (ext #105)	16	12
107	Trombone (from #78)	16	—
108	Bassoon (from #73)	16	—
109	Tromba (ext #107)	8	12
110	Clarion (ext #109)	4	12

GALLERY ORGAN

ANTIPHONAL

111	Open Diapason	8	61
112	Principal	4	61
113	Hooded Trumpet	8	61

ECHO (ENCLOSED)

114	Chimney Flute	8	61
115	Viola di Gamba (1-7 from #114)	8	54
116	Flute	4	61
	Tremulant		
	Zimbelstern		

PEDAL

117	Bourdon (ext #114)	16	12
118	Octavebass (1-10 from #111)	8	22

Gallery Couplers
(draw knobs)
Antiphonal, Echo to Pedal
Pedal main off
Antiphonal, Echo to Great
Great main off
Antiphonal, Echo to Choir
Choir main off

COUPLERS (IN TABLETS)

Great, Swell, Choir, Orch.
Bombarde, to Pedal Unison
Swell, Bombarde to Pedal Super
Swell, Choir to Great Sub,
Unison, Super
Orch to Great Sub, Unison
Swell, Orch. to Choir Sub,
Unison, Super
Orch. to Swell Sub, Unison, Super
Bombarde to Great, Choir Unison
Great Super

Swell Sub, Super
Choir Sub, Super
Orch. Sup, Super
Echo to Antiphonal

ADJUSTABLE COMBINATION PISTONS

Artisan-Classic System 99 levels
Great, Swell, Choir, Orch, Pedal 8
thumb pistons
Bombarde 3 thumb pistons
General 8 thumb pistons, 8
General Toe pistons
Antiphonal Echo
General Cancel
Adjuster

REVERSIBLE PISTONS

Great to Pedal thumb and toe
Swell, Choir, Orch. Bomb. to
Pedal thumb
Swell, Choir, Orch to Great
thumb
Swell to Choir thumb
Great and Swell combination
coupler
reversers in Great and Swell key
cheeks
Full Organ toe.

ACTION

Electro-pneumatic Pitman type
Reservoir winding.

ANALYSIS

	STOPS	RANKS	PIPES	REAL STOPS
Great	23	29	1892	23
Swell	19	26	1749	19
Choir	22	25	1482	22
Orch.	19	22	1428	19
Bomb.	6	12	732	6
Gallery	8	7	393	7
Pedal	23	10	416	7
Totals	120	131	8092	103

The terraced console of the organ at Our Lady of Sorrows is 'attached' to the Ruckpositiv at the organist's back and 'detached' from the main organ. The trackers for the Great Organ run horizontally for about twelve feet and are kept straight with hangers to avoid lost motion at the keys.

CHURCH OF OUR LADY OF SORROWS

3055 Bloor Street West
Casavant Organ, Opus 2805, 1965

Etobicoke, which recently became a part of the City of Toronto through an act of the Government of Ontario, is itself an amalgam of several communities which, when the municipal council of the Township of Etobicoke was established in 1850, were thriving villages.

The first two churches in Etobicoke were Anglican: St. Philip's at the north end of Royal York Road and Christ Church near the south end, established in the late 1820s. In 1856, St. Patrick's Church was established on Dundas Street at Dixie Road. This was the church which served Etobicoke until 1881, when the mission church of St. Joseph was established to serve the Catholic community within the boundaries of what is now Our Lady of Sorrows parish. In 1913, a second mission of St. Patrick's, known as St. Rita's, became established in a former Odd Fellows Hall near the intersection of Dundas Street and Prince Edward Road, and served the Roman Catholics of the area for the next 10 years.

By the time the Humber Valley Estates were being developed in Kingsway Park and the Old Mill areas in 1925, the nearest Catholic Parish was that of St. James' located on Annette Street near Jane Street. The Reverend Gregory F. Kelly, the pastor of St. James,' requested permission from Archbishop (later Cardinal) James C. McGuigan to establish a new parish which would serve this new residential area growing to the west of the Humber River.

Although the parish was formally established on

March 26, 1940, a search for an appropriate site for a new church had begun the previous fall. Since that November, Father Kelly had also been working with Toronto architect James H. Haffa, K.S.G., M.R.A.I.C. to develop an appropriate architecture for the new house of worship.

The architect's written design proposal for the "Church of Our Mother of Sorrows" read as follows:

"To me there are only three styles of architecture – Greek or Architecture of the lintel; Romanesque or Architecture of the round arch; and Gothic or Architecture of the gable…"
"Romanesque falls into two great branches – Eastern and Western, or Byzantine and Lombardic…. We chose the Lombardy style…"

Building permits were issued by the Ontario Department of Highways in April 1940. World War II had begun, and it is of interest to note that the steel used in the church's construction was the last available for non-war use in the Toronto region.

By December of the same year the new edifice was fit to be blessed by Archbishop McGuigan, assisted by other officials of the church.

Compared to the rich interior that we know today, the church of 1940 would have been quite stark. The beautification of the church was the contribution of

The Casavant Organ at Our Lady of Sorrows Church. The largest pipes of the Pedal Untersatz 16′ lie horizontally below the main pedal chest within the casework. The pipes of the façade are of seventy-five percent polished tin. They all speak but one.

Msgr. F.V. Allen, D.D.,V.G., Bishop and Vicar General of the Diocese of Toronto during his tenure as pastor of Our Lady of Sorrows. He was a great admirer of beauty and art in churches. Alterations and decorations were completed in early 1961.

The exterior massing and detailing of the church is characteristic of an architecture which blossomed in Lombardy in the eleventh century, having originated in the area around Milan and then developing in the Rhineland. In the interior we experience a space which, with its coffered ceiling, applied marbles, rich mosaics and inscriptions, is more representative of a 15th century Renaissance church. The room measures 42 metres (138 feet) in length, 23 metres (75 feet) in width, comprising nave and two aisles, and 11 metres (36 feet) in height.

It was also Bishop Allen who undertook to build the choir and in the early 1960s championed the installation of a new Casavant Frères tracker organ in the rear gallery of the church. The Curate, Rev. John Mott, was an organist and former choirboy at St. Simon's Anglican Church, Toronto.

This is the first modern example of a fully Reformed organ in Ontario, an organ with mechanical key action, each division separately encased and with open toe, un-nicked, low pressure pipes in classical form. It is possibly the first organ in Ontario to have a Rückpositiv, an organ set at the back of the organist and hung from the gallery rail.

Father Mott visited Lawrence Phelps, Tonal Director of Casavant Frères at a time when the building of tracker organs was being revived in a corner of the plant. Karl Wilhelm and Hellmuth Wolff guided the design and production of the first two dozen instruments. The 200th modern, Casavant tracker organ was built in 1987. The Sorrows organ, assigned to Wolff, was the 14th modern tracker organ. The cost of the organ at $37,500.00 was only one tenth of the cost of the recently completed decorative tiles in the upper walls and ceiling of the church. Father Mott wanted mechanical action, but placement was a problem. Six winged angels pictured flying toward the rose window in the rear gallery were going to be left with their feet and trains sticking out from behind the organ cases. But once the Bishop saw J.C. Gauthier's drawing, all was well. The memorial window was left showing by splitting the main casework, Great on the left, and Pedal on the right. The angels went behind a layer of gold tile.

By the time the Organ Reform Movement reached North America, European builders had done ten years of research and innovation, replacing the bombed organs with new tracker instruments. The self-adjusting floating fulcrum gave every organ a key touch that stayed constant. Modern glues and high quality laminated wood overcame the cracking and running suffered by every 19th century Toronto tracker organ. All sorts of small parts went into production. Frictionless pivots of steel and moulded plastic clips replaced handmade wooden parts. The key action of the new tracker organs was suddenly a delight to play. The very pluck of the chest pallet against the wind pressure could be sensed at the key twenty feet away. Even the closing of the pallet could be sensed. With such an instrument, the organist had more control over the attack of the pipes than harpsichordists had with their plectra and strings. The tracker organ was back to stay.

The Sorrows organ was much used by the English organist Peter Hurford for his recordings of pre-nineteenth century music for Argo and Decca.

Casavant Organ, Opus 2805, 1965

GREAT ORGAN		FEET	PIPES
1	Prinzipal	8	56
2	Rohrflöte	8	56
3	Oktave	4	56
4	Waldflöte	4	56
5	Nasat	2-2/3	56
6	Superoktave	2	56
7	Mixtur V	1-1/3	280
8	Trompete	8	56

POSITIV ORGAN			
9	Holzgedackt	8	56
10	Salizional	8	56
11	Prinzipal	4	56
12	Rohrquintade	4	56
13	Gemshorn	2	56
14	Sifflöte	1	56
15	Sesquialtera II	2-2/3	56
16	Scharff IV	1	224
17	Musette	8	56
	Tremulant		

PEDAL ORGAN			
18	Untersatz	16	32
19	Oktavbass	8	32
20	Pommer	8	32
21	Choralbass	4	32
22	Nachthorn	2	32
23	Rauschpfeife III	2	96
24	Fagott	16	32
25	Klarine	4	32

COUPLERS (TOE LEVERS)
Great to Pedal 8
Postiv to Pedal 8
Positiv to Great 8

ACTION
Mechanical key and stop action

ROSEDALE PRESBYTERIAN CHURCH

129 Mount Pleasant Road
Karl Wilhelm Inc. Organ, 1982

The exclusive Toronto neighborhood of Rosedale was first deeded to Captain George Playter in 1796 as a 200-acre farm. By 1924 a 120-acre portion of the property had been sold to William Botsford Jarvis, who was appointed High Sheriff of the Home District. Here he built an estate for his wife and family, naming it "Rosedale" for the wild roses that bloomed on the property. The approach to Rosedale was from Yonge Street, crossing a simple bridge over the ravine and climbing steeply to the house.

In 1837 Sheriff Jarvis became a hero when he successfully defended Toronto from rebels. In 1853 Jarvis sold most of the estate to a developer who registered a plan to have 100 acres divided into 72 lots. Until this time, Jarvis and Sherbourne Streets were the preferred addresses of the well-to-do. Rosedale soon became the respected address for the monied.

Rosedale Presbyterian Church is located on South Drive at Mount Pleasant Road. It was constructed in 1909-10 to a design by architects Chapman & McGiffin. Alfred Chapman was a Torontonian who did his training with E. Beaumont Jarvis and Burke and Horwood before heading off to study at the Ecole des Beaux-Arts in Montreal and then to work in New York City. He returned in 1907 and immediately got the contract for the Toronto Public Reference Library, now the Koffler Student Services Centre of the University of Toronto, on College Street. Rosedale Presbyterian Church followed on the heels of this project. He went on to practice for some thirty years and produced a number of fine buildings in a variety of historical styles. For example, both the east wing of the Royal Ontario Museum and Holy Blossom Temple, designed in the 1930s, are executed in a late Romanesque style.

In Rosedale Presbyterian Church, Toronto saw one of its earlier examples of the Modern Gothic style. The edifice was built as a first-phase chapel of a complex which was to have included a larger church to the west. With church union in 1925, and the reported loss of almost two-fifths of its members, these plans were put in question. By 1948 a portion of the west end of the property was required for the widening of Huntley Street to become Mount Pleasant Road. The concept of a larger church was

abandoned. In 1955, the remaining buildable site area was developed to provide additional space for church educational facilities, and not the larger church.

Since it was intended to be a provisional worship space, Chapman included some interesting planning features to accommodate over-flow seating. The main axis of the nave and choir is augmented by a second one, at right angles forming a crossing. At the crossing, on a raised platform with a hardwood floor, is the "table," and on it a three-dimensional brass cross by the Barrie artist, Don Stuart. One cannot be sure what John Calvin would have thought of the arrangement.

The secondary axis, when it crosses the main axis, forms a shallow transept towards the east which now accommodates the Karl Wilhelm organ. To the west, this secondary axis becomes, on the main level, a secondary seating area which was designed to be partitioned off to be a church parlour. Above this is a deep balcony which is separated by a folding partition and is now used as a Board Room.

Dr. Robert Hubbard, in a Bulletin of the National Gallery of Canada published in 1975, felt that the architecture of the church was "less successful on the interior because of a small cluttered chancel." This clutter was largely the result of the church having purchased an organ built for another church, which resulted in a very crowded installation. This instrument was an electrified D. W. Karn organ of 14 stops, and played from a two-manual, Casavant console built in

The Karl Wilhelm Organ in Rosedale Presbyterian Church. The hand-operated doors protect the Brustwerk pipes from tampering and can also be used to protect the ears of the organist.

1952. As usual with Karn organs, the top notes cyphered every winter.

With its high plaster walls, hardwood flooring, timbered ceiling and rich oak woodwork, today the church is elegant and acoustically satisfying, in spite of its small proportions. Word has it that the area of pews in the west transept, facing the organ, is the preferred seating.

Karl Wilhelm Inc., 1982

HAUPTWERK		FEET	PIPES
1	Bourdon	16	56
2	Prinzipal	8	56
3	Rohrflöte	8	56
4	Oktave	4	56
5	Spitzflöte	4	56
6	Superoktave	2	56
7	Mixtur IV	1-1/3	224
8	Trompette	8	56

BRUSTWERK			
(HAND OPERATED SHADES)			
9	Holzgedackt	8	56
10	Rohrflöte	8	56
11	Quinte	2-2/3	56
12	Doublette	2	56
13	Terz	1-3/5	56
14	Zimbel III	2/3	168
15	Regal	8	56
	Tremolo		

PEDAL			
16	Subbass	16	30
17	Oktavbass	8	30
18	Choralbass	4	30
19	Fagott	16	30
20	Posaune	8	30

COUPLERS
Hauptwerk, Brustwerk to Pedal
Brustwerk to Hauptwerk

View of the Roy Thomson Hall audience from the position of the organist seated at the tracker console. Visual interest is provided at the ceiling by Quebec fabric artist, Mariette Rousseau Vermette's four thousand tapestried cylinders which were intended to provide the possibility of adjusting the reverberation of the hall.

ROY THOMSON HALL

60 Simcoe Street
Gabriel Kney, Pipe Organ Builders, London, Ontario
Opus 95, 1981

The Gabriel Kney Organ at Roy Thomson Hall. The Pedal Organ is mainly in the left side of the case and the Hauptwerk on the right. In the centre is the Brustwerk just above the console, the Swell above that, the Trompeteria above that set out in minor thirds then the Positiv at the top.

Roy Thomson Hall was the first 20th century public concert hall in Canada, since the Eaton Auditorium, conceived to feature a pipe organ. As home to the Toronto Symphony Orchestra and the Toronto Mendelssohn Choir, such an instrument was intended to expand the orchestral repertoire to include such works as the Camille Saint-Saëns Symphony No. 3, as well as to provide the ideal underpinning to many oratorio and other choral works.

It is no secret that the hall has not been an acoustical success and plans are being made to rebuild the interior of the hall during the summer of 2002. There is hope in some corners that the organ may also become a winner in these plans, because at the moment the hall and organ have not been a good match for each other. By all accounts, the appearance of the hall will change significantly, which makes this description of the original design of particular value.

For the design of their new hall, the Board of Directors of Massey Hall (the two halls are one organization) chose the great contemporary Canadian architect, Arthur Erickson. Erickson had first caught the world's attention in 1965 with his concept for Simon Fraser University, which in many ways followed the antecedents of the Greek acropolis. Ten years later, for the Toronto commission, his assignment was to replicate the listener/performer relationship for the same size of audience and warm acoustics of historic Massey Hall, but in more spacious and modern surroundings.

The design process, therefore, began with the seating. It then proceeded to determine the correct shape for a building that would relate both to the seating and to the site constraints. The architect built thirty-two models before finding an acceptable solution, and then, once costs and some of the technical concerns were addressed, even this scheme had to be modified.

A building that today reads as an overturned galvanized washtub was to be a more beautiful and complex shape; the reflective curtain of glass was to transform from an elliptical roof to the edge of the square podium.

Inside, Erickson exposed the bare bones of the structural concrete cage which both supports the multiple balconies required to keep 3,300 members of the audience within an acceptable distance of the performers, and provides the acoustical mass required to protect the audience from street noise. Other materials required by the composition – the flooring, doors, and seating – were selected to blend with the warm gray tones of the concrete, creating "a quiet background that lets the audience supply most of the colour."[1]

Even the organ case had to be constructed to Erickson's minimalist design and colour scheme. In 1978 Gabriel Kney developed a preliminary design concept, a classic wooden *werkprincipe*, for the organ, which was rejected by the architect.

In the end it was Erickson who provided Kney with the visuals that he wanted, giving Kney free rein as to the construction and tonal design. The look of the completed organ thrills some and disappoints others. The three-story, totally rectilinear case, though made of wood, has been painted with a glossy silver paint (actually automotive enamel) which gives the shimmering effect that Erickson wanted. Transparent perspex has been used for the expression shutters.

There are two consoles. The one with mechanical key action is at the base of the organ, one level above the choir loft of the hall. The second is a movable console at stage level which controls the instrument through a detachable cable. The coupler and combination action was built by Solid State Logic, Oxford.

The manual key action employs pneumatic assist. The single pallet for each note is opened either by a pull-down, latch magnet or directly with a wire tracker operating a floating lever. The trackers throughout the organ are of wire rather than wood. The stop action sliders are solenoid driven. A safety harness is used by the tuner when reaching upward to the horizontal pipes of the Trompeteria.

Roy Thomson Hall has not often been sought as a venue for organ concerts, but this might change after 2002 when acoustical improvements are completed. It was obvious from the beginning that the organ could not cope with the large space and dry acoustic.

1. *Seven Stones: A Portrait of Arthur Erickson Architect*, Edith Iglauer

GABRIEL KNEY, PIPE ORGAN BUILDERS, LONDON, ONTARIO OPUS 95, 1981

HAUPTWERK (MAN. II)	FEET	PIPES
1 Praestant		
(1, 2 from #58)	16	56
2 Bourdon	16	58
3 Oktav	8	58
4 Rohrflöte	8	58
5 Gross Nasat	5-1/3	58
6 Oktav	4	58
7 Spitzflöte	4	58
8 Gross Tierce	3-1/5	58
9 Quint	2-2/3	58
10 Oktav	2	58
11 Mixtur V	2	290
12 Scharff IV	2/3	232
13 Cornet V TenF – c49	8	160
14 Trompete	16	58
15 Trompete	8	58

POSITIV (MAN. I)		
16 Pommer	16	58
17 Praestant	8	58
18 Gedeckt	8	58
19 Quintadena	8	58
20 Oktav	4	58
21 Flachflöte	4	58
22 Nasat	2-2/3	58
23 Oktav	2	58
24 Blockflöte	2	58
25 Tierce	1-3/5	58
26 Larigot	1-1/3	58
27 Terzian II	1-3/5	116
28 Scharff IV	1	232
29 Rankett-Dulzian	16	58
30 Krummhorn	8	58
Tremulant		
Zimbelstern 8 bells		

SWELL ORGAN (MAN. III) (ENCLOSED)		
31 Hohlflöte	8	58
32 Salicional	8	58
33 Céleste (TenA)	8	50
34 Prinzipal	4	58
35 Koppelflöte	4	58
36 Flauto veneziano	2	58
37 Oktav	1	58
38 Sesquialter II		
Ten C	2-2/3	92
39 Fourniture IV	2	232
40 Zimbel III	1/2	174
41 Basson	16	58
42 Trompette	8	58
43 Hautbois	8	58
44 Clairon	4	58
Tremulant		

BRUSTWERK (MAN. IV) (ENCLOSED)		
45 Holzgedackt	8	58
46 Erzahler	8	58
47 Erzahler céleste TenC	8	46
48 Offenflöte	4	58
49 Prinzipal	2	58
50 Sifflöte	1	58
51 Terzimbel III	2/3	174
52 Musette	16	58
53 Voix Humaine	8	58
54 Rohrschalmey	4	58
Tremulant		

TROMPETERIA (FLOATING ELECTRIC ACTION)		
55 Bajoncillo (bass)	4	25
Tompeta magna (treble)	16	33
56 Trompeta Batalla (bass)	8	25
Trompeta Batalla (treble)	8	33

PEDAL

57	Untersatz	32	12
58	Prinzipal	16	32
59	Subbass	16	32
60	Quintbass	10-2/3	32
61	Oktav	8	32
62	Gedacktbass	8	32
63	Choralbass	4	32
64	Koppelflöte	4	32
65	Nachthorn	2	32
66	Hintersatz IV	5-1/3	128
67	Mixture VI	2-2/3	192
68	Bombarde	32	12
69	Posaune	16	32
70	Trompete	8	32
71	Schalmey	4	32

COUPLERS (MECHANICAL)
Sw/Ped, Hw/Ped, Pos/Ped, Tr/Ped,
Bw/Sw
Tr/Hw, Tr/Pos, Tr/Sw, Tr/Bw

(ELECTRIC AND MECHANICAL)
Sw/Hw, Pos/Hw

ADJUSTABLE COMBINATION PISTONS
(SSL 2 levels A,B)
6 Thumb Pistons to Hw, Sw, Pos,
Br
6 Thumb & Toe Pistons to Ped
12 Thumb & Toe Generals
Adjuster and General Cancel
Thumb

REVERSABLE PISTONS

Hw, Sw, Pos/Ped	Thumb
Sw, Hw/Ped	Toe
Sw, Pos/Hw	Thumb & Toe
Sw/Pos	Thumb
Full Organ	Thumb & Toe

One Adjustable Toe Piston to I, II,
III, Ped.

One of the ironies of the site planning of Roy Thomson Hall is that the architect tried to divorce the hall from Toronto's King Street West entertainment district, rather that be a part of it. A sunken garden with a reflecting pool provides a "moat" of protection from neighbouring theatres offering lighter fare. This pixel sign and over-stated poster cases have been a recent attempt to draw in some of the King Street pedestrian traffic.

SAINT ANDREW'S EVANGELICAN LUTHERAN CHURCH

383 Jarvis Street
Casavant Organ Opus 618, 1915
Rebuild of S. R. Warren Organ
Tonally revised, 1984

The original casework of the S. R. Warren tracker organ at St. Andrew's Evangelical Lutheran Church remains. The pipes not showing mouths were added in 1915 to screen the larger instrument.

The story of how the two St. Andrew's churches featured in this book came to share a name is a fascinating one. Until 1876, the congregations of the two churches were one, worshipping together since 1830 in the first St. Andrew's Church located on the south-west corner of Church and Adelaide Streets.

By 1873 the Presbyterian congregation had outgrown a building and some of the members felt that available funds should be used to erect a new church rather than restore the old building. A new building was erected at the westerly end of town, at the corner of King and Simcoe Streets, which continues to be known as St. Andrew's Presbyterian Church. A total of 72 dissenters, including 58 active members of the church, petitioned the Presbytery of Toronto to permit them to organize a second congregation under the name "Old St. Andrew's." This group was eventually permitted to remain in the first building under their requested name.

The construction of the church at the corner of Jarvis and Carlton Streets is very much tied to the ministry of Rev. George MacBeth Milligan, who would only accept a call to minister to the people of Old St. Andrew's if they would agree to purchase a property on fashionable Jarvis Street and construct a new church building.

The new "Old St. Andrew's Church" was completed in 1878. Designed by the firm of Langley & Burke, the church was described by John Ross Robertson, a member of the church, in his 1904 book, *Landmarks of Toronto*, as follows:

The style is second-pointed Gothic; the material is reddish-grey Credit Valley freestone, with Ohio stone dressing; the roof ornamented with foliations in slate, with neat iron cresting. Particularly noticeable are the doors and windows, affording examples of the perfect beauty and grace of Gothic architecture. The building being devoid of special ornamentation and elaboration, does not afford opportunities of real artistic effects, but whatever of plainness characterizes it in this way is amply atoned for in the symmetry and harmony of its construction. It presents a uniform, substantial, real appearance that fittingly symbolizes the character of the religious faith in which it is enshrined. The interior is amphitheatrical in form, gracefully canopied with groined arches 36 feet above the floor, supported by two iron piers. It will conveniently seat 900…The woodwork is in butternut, with dark walnut mouldings and caps…..the three fine, large, triple windows light the auditorium very clearly…There are two entrances underneath the towers on Jarvis Street.

Much has remained unchanged. At the time of church union in 1925, the church became St. Andrew's United Church, and in 1951 the building was sold to the Evangelical Lutheran Synod of Canada to serve an Estonian and a Latvian congregation, who have since maintained and improved the building for their worship.

Most noteworthy changes include the moving of the choir to the gallery, the repositioning of the organ console to the south side of the nave, and the installation of an altar of Italian marble and a new wooden communion rail supported by balusters in front of the historic high pulpit and beautifully worked organ screen. In 1989 the windows were replaced by a stunningly beautiful set of leaded glass designed by the Lutz Haufschild of Breslau, Germany. These windows have no equal in the City of Toronto.

Signs of the Orchestral era abound in the editing of the stop list and instructions to the organ builder. The traditional Harmonic Flute 8' on the Great was crossed out and changed to a Tibia Minor 8'. The Pedal Violone 16' was to be "slim & stringy, new pipes" and the Vox Humana "must be extra fine & new." The Celesta is a genuine Mustel instrument made in Paris, France with an electro-pneumatic action for moving the keys.

Each division contains a number of stops on high wind pressure (7") requiring an extra reservoir for each organ: Great, Swell, Choir and Pedal.

The Great Organ was built with two separate key primary actions controlling the "G" or Grave chest and the "A" or Aigue chest. The "A" chest was affected by the Super coupler but not the Sub coupler. The "G" chest was affected by the Sub couplers but not the Super couplers.

The case is the original Warren case but with extra pipes added to screen the much-enlarged organ of 1915.

ORIGIN, REVISIONS, REPAIRS

18?? Samuel R. Warren organ built

1915 Casavant Opus 618 organ built for "Old St. Andrew's Church" with electro-pneumatic action, Ventil chests using ranks of pipes and casework from previous S. R. Warren Organ.

19?? Date unknown, organ action partly re-leathered.

1968 Organ cleaned, original Casavant, hand-wound, wood-capped magnets replaced.

1973 Façade repainted, previously gilded.

1974 Console moved from central position below pulpit to side location.

1977-80 Blower repaired

1983 Great Main and Tuba reservoirs re-covered

1984 Tonal revisions to Choir Organ, new Gedackt 8, Zimbel III, Quinte 1-1/3, Swell Organ and Pedal chests re-leathered. Swell flues re-voiced, reeds cut dead-length and cleaned.

1986 Upper and lower Swell reservoirs re-covered. Tonal revisions to Great Organ, new Cornet III, Zimbel III, Mixture revised, flues re-voiced, Tromba re-voiced with new tongues, cut dead length.

1993 Upper and lower Choir reservoirs re-covered.

1995 Pedal reed and main reservoirs and Great main low pressure reservoir re-covered.

1998 Swell distributor re-leathered.

Casavant Organ Opus 619, 1915
Rebuild of S. R. Warren Organ
Tonally revised, 1984

GREAT ORGAN		FEET	PIPES
1	Double Open Diapason	16	61
2	Diapason	8	61
3	Principal	8	61
4	Tibia Minor	8	61
5	Rohrflöte	8	61
6†	Principal	4	61
7†	Harmonic Flute	4	61
8	Twelfth	2-2/3	61
9†	Fifteenth	2	61
10*	Cornet Ten C	III	147
11†	Mixture	IV	244
12*	Zimbel	III	183
13	Tromba	8	61
	Celesta		
	49 bars, lower 12 repeat		

SWELL ORGAN (ENCLOSED)			
14†	Bourdon	16	61
15†	Diapason	8	61
16†	Stopped Diapason	8	61
17†	Viola di Gamba	8	61
18†	Voix céleste Ten C	8	49
19†	Aeoline	8	61
20†	Octave	4	61
21	Flauto Traverso	4	61
22	Flageolet	2	61
23	Mixture	III	183
24	Contra Posaune	16	61
25	Posaune	8	61
26†	Oboe	8	61
27	Vox Humana	8	61
28	Clarion	4	61
	Tremulant		
	Celesta (from Great)		

CHOIR ORGAN (ENCLOSED)			
29	Contra Viola	16	61
30*	Gedackt	8	61
31	Principal	4	61
32†	Flute	4	61
33†	Piccolo	2	61
34*	Quinte	1-1/3	61
35*	Zimbel	III	183
36	Viole d'Orchestra (high pressure)	8	61
37	Clarinet	8	61
38	Tuba high pressure	8	61
	Tremulant		
	Celesta (from Great)		

PEDAL ORGAN			
39	Resultant (from #41, #43)	32	—
40	Open Diapason (metal)(from #1)	16	—
41	Open Diapason (wood)	16	30
42	Violone	16	30
43	Bourdon	16	30
44	Gedackt (from #14)	16	—
45	Principal	8	30
46	Stopped Diapason (ext #43)	8	12
47	Octave (ext #45)	4	12
48	Trombone	16	30
49	Posaune (ext #48)	8	12

COUPLERS
Great, Swell, Choir/Pedal   8
Swell, Choir/Pedal   4
Swell/Great   16, 8, 4
Choir/Great   16, 8, 4
Great/Great   16, 4
Swell/Swell   16, 8 off, 4
Swell/Choir   16, 8, 4
Choir/Choir   16, 8 off, 4

ADJUSTABLE COMBINATIONS
(CAPTURE SYSTEM)
Great   1 2 3 4   Thumb
Swell   1 2 3 4 5   Thumb
Choir   1 2 3 4   Thumb
Pedal   1 2 3 4   Toe
General   1 2 3 4   Toe
General Cancel   Thumb
Adjuster   Thumb

REVERSIBLE PISTONS
Great / Pedal   Thumb and toe
Swell, Choir/Pedal   Thumb
Swell, Choir/Great   Thumb
Swell / Choir   Thumb
Full Organ   Toe
Swell, Choir Tremulants   Toe

ANALYSIS

	STOPS	RANKS	PIPES	REAL STOPS
Great	13	20	1184	13
Swell	15	17	1025	15
Choir	10	12	732	10
Pedal	11	6	216	6
Totals	49	55	3157	44

*new pipes, 1984
†S.R.Warren pipes

One of a complete set of leaded glass designed and installed by the German artist, Lutz Haufschild.

61

SAINT ANDREW'S PRESBYTERIAN CHURCH

73 Simcoe Street
S. R. Warren 1884, Casavant Organ Opus 300, 1907,
Console 1938; Karl Wilhelm Inc., 1983

(Opposite, left, bottom) St. Andrew's Presbyterian Church was built in 1873 to a design of the architect William Storm.

(Above) One of the twin cases of Casavant Organ Opus 300, 1907 in the chancel. The façade pipes have Roman upper and lower lips and pipe decoration made to match
that of the Warren Gallery Organ (Opposite, top left).

(Opposite) The new Karl Wilhelm Organ in the Gallery of St. Andrew's Presbyterian Church. Elements from the 1884 Warren Organ casework stand at the side. Pipes of the Warren 32' Contra Bourdon stand against the rear wall.

"Education, Legislation, Salvation and Damnation" was how the intersection of King and Simcoe Streets was known after the building of the current St. Andrew's Church. St. Andrew's Church, of course, represents Salvation. Upper Canada College, representing Education, was located kitty-corner, north of King Street and west of Simcoe Street. On the current site of Roy Thomson Hall was located the French Renaissance mansion of the Lieutenant Governor and on the remaining corner a saloon. Today, of the four, only Salvation remains.

A number of designs were received in response to a competition announced by the Building Committee in 1873. Of these a design by William G. Storm was selected because the "Norman Scottish" style was felt to reflect the Church of Scotland heritage of the congregation. William Storm had learned the profession in the office of William Thomas. As the licensed apprentice of Thomas, architect of St. Michael's Roman Catholic Cathedral, Storm had had the advantage of a number of trips to England and France where he had shared Thomas' enthusiasm for the Norman Style.

While the church is an outstanding example of Norman Romanesque Revival architecture, a flanking tower is built in the Scottish Baronial style topped with four conical bartizans and stepped gables.

Inside we find a room which has warmth in spite of its size. The rich, ruby-colored cherry wood used for many of the fittings contributes to this feeling. A horseshoe-shaped balcony is supported by "barley-twisted" supporting columns. These columns, as well as an intricate balustrade, are formed in cast iron. The chancel was added in 1907, as was the second organ, and a central aisle was introduced for the first time.

A gently sloping floor provides a clear line of vision to a grand pulpit and the voluminous chancel area. The new organ was installed in the gallery in 1983, and the choir was moved to be near the organ, emphatically creating a void in the chancel.

The lower chords of the timber scissor trusses are visible below the plaster, but these intricately carved wood members do not likely have a great impact on the acoustic of the room. It is rather due to the continuous balcony that the room is not as resonant as an organist would like. Sound-reflecting sidewalls are thus broken. Sound becomes trapped below the balcony and dies.

The Karl Wilhelm organ follows closely the classical principles of tone and placement. It stands free in two cases of solid wood which serve to blend and focus the sound. The Grand Orgue is central above the impost with the Pédale divided either side. The Positif is just above the console and the Récit is in a separate case behind the main structure. The Pédale Soubasse 32′ pipes are set against the back wall. They are pipes from the Warren organ of 1884. Portions of the casework trim from the previous S. R. Warren organ are displayed at either side of the gallery.

S. R. Warren organ, 1884
rear gallery, removed 1982

GREAT ORGAN

‡ *	Bourdon	16
‡	Open Diapason	8
*	Gamba	8
‡	Doppel Flute	8
‡	Dolce	8
‡	Principal	4
‡	Flute d'Amour	4
‡*	Twelfth	2-2/3
‡*	Fifteenth	2
*	Acuta II	2/3
*	Sesquialtera III	1-3/5
‡*	Posaune	8
*	Clarion	4

SWELL ORGAN (ENCLOSED)

	Bourdon	16
‡	Open Diapason	8
‡	Aeoline	8
‡	Viole di Gamba	8
‡	Quintadena	8
‡	Gedackt	8
‡	Octave	4
‡	Traverse Flute	4
	Superoctave	2
‡	Mixture	III
‡	Krummhorn	16
‡	Horn	8
‡	Oboe	8
‡	Vox Humana	8
	Clarion	4
	Tremulant	

CHOIR ORGAN (ENCLOSED)

	Lieblich Gedackt	16
	Geigen Principal	8
	Melodia	8
	Dulciana	8
	Fugara	4
	Flute Harmonique	4
	Piccolo	2

	Contra Faggotto	
	Ten C	16
	Corno di Bassetto	
	TenC	8
	Tremulant	

PEDAL ORGAN

	Contra Bourdon	32
‡	Open Diapason	16
‡	Bourdon	16
‡	Violone	16
‡	Violoncello	8
‡	Bass Flute	8
‡	Trombone	16

Key action mechanical, chest action pneumatic

*enclosed with Choir
‡ stops playable from 1938
 console

It was generally believed that the S. R. Warren organ in St. Andrew's gallery was a tracker-action organ. If it had been, it might have survived along with its neighbour, the three-manual Warren of 1880 in St. Michael's Cathedral which was still in regular use in 1993 when the gallery was closed. The St. Andrew's organ had tracker-action keyboards but not the usual pallet and slider chests. The trackers were only used to trip the pneumatics much in the same way that the lead tubes of (the new) tubular organs operated primary and secondary valves of the pneumatic wind chests.

In order to connect the Gallery Organ to play with the new Chancel Casavant in 1907, electro-pneumatic action was fitted to pull down the trackers. The same action was connected to the new console in 1938 but within ten years the Gallery Organ was cyphering badly and the wind was finally turned off. Attempts made during the tenure of Giles Bryant to revive the organ were not successful.

Casavant Organ Opus 300, 1907, Chancel Organ

electro-pneumatic action added to play Gallery Organ. New console built 1938

Great Organ		Feet	Pipes
1	Open Diapason (1-2 from #38)	16	59
2	Open Diapason I	8	61
3	Violin Diapason	8	61
4	Doppel Flute	8	61
5	Dolce	8	61
6	Principal	4	61
7	Harmonic Flute	4	61
8	Fifteenth	2	61
9	Mixture	III	183
10	Trumpet	8	61
	Gongs		
	Great 4 Coupler		

Gallery Great Organ

10 stops (‡) and Super Coupler

Swell Organ (enclosed)			
11	Bourdon	16	61
12	Horn Diapason	8	61
13	Stopped Diapason	8	61
14	Gamba	8	61
15	Voix celeste	8	na
16	Dulcissimo	8	61
17	Principal	4	61
18	Traverse Flute	4	61
19	Piccolo	2	61
20	Cornet	III	183
21	Cornopean	8	61
22	Oboe	8	61
23	Vox Humana	8	61
	Tremulant		

Gongs
Swell 16, 4 Couplers

Gallery Swell

(13 stops (‡) Sub, Super, Trem.)

Choir Organ (enclosed)			
24	Geigen Diapason	8	61
25	Melodia	8	61
26	Dulciana	8	61
27	Wald Flute	4	61
28	Violina	4	61
29	Flageolet	2	61
30	Clarinet	8	61
	Tremulant		

Choir 16, 4 Couplers
Gongs

Solo Organ (enclosed)			
31	Gross Flute	8	61
32	Cello	8	61
33	Viole d'Orchestre	8	61
34	Tuba	8	61
35	Cor Anglais	8	61
	Tremulant		

Solo 16, 4 Couplers
Gongs

Pedal Organ			
36	Open Diapason	16	30
37	Violone	16	30
38	Bourdon	16	30
39	Lieblich Gedackt (Sw)	16	—
40	Stopped Diapason (ext #38)	8	12
41	Trombone	16	30
42	Trumpet (ext #41)	8	12

Gallery Pedal Organ

(6 stops (‡))

Couplers (in tablets)

Great, Swell, Choir, Solo/Pedal 16, 8, 4
Swell, Choir, Solo/Great 16, 8, 4
Swell/Choir 16, 8, 4
Solo/Swell, Choir 8
Choir 8 off
Gallery On, Chancel Off
Gallery On
Crescendo Reverser

Gallery Great, Swell/Pedal 8, 4
Gallery Swell/Great 16, 8, 4

Adjustable Pistons, capture type
Action electro-pneumatic, Ventil chests

When opened in 1907, the Chancel organ of 44 stops, 49 ranks combined with the Gallery Organ of 27 stops, 29 ranks would combine as 71 stops, 78 ranks and was probably the second largest organ in Toronto.

Karl Wilhelm Inc. Opus 57, 1983

Grand Orgue		Feet	Pipes
1	Bourdon	16	56
2	Montre	8	56
3	Bourdon	8	56
4	Prestant	4	56
5	Flûte Conique		56
6	Gross Tierce	3-1/5	56
7	Nazard	2-2/3	56
8	Doublette	2	56
9	Tierce	1-3/5	56
10	Fourniture IV	1-1/3	224
11	Cymbale III	2/3	168
12	Cornet V Ten c	8	220
13	Trompette	8	56
14	Voix humaine	8	56
15	Clairon	4	56

Récit (enclosed)			
16	Principal (1-7 from #17)	8	49
17	Bourdon	8	56
18	Gambe	8	56
19	Céleste Ten c	8	44
20	Prestant	4	56
21	Flûte	4	56
22	Flageolet	2	56
23	Cornet III	2	183
24	Plein jeu IV	2	183
25	Basson	16	56
26	Trompette	8	56
27	Hautbois	8	56
	Tremblant		
	Rossignol		
	Zimbelstern		

Positif			
28	Dessus de flûte	8	56
29	Flûte à cheminé	8	56
30	Montre	4	56
31	Flûte à fuseau	4	56
32	Nazard	2-2/3	56
33	Quarte de nazard	2	56
34	Doublette	2	56
35	Tierce	1-3/5	56
36	Larigot	1-1/3	56
37	Cymbale IV	1	224
38	Cromorne	8	56
	Tremulant		

Pédale			
39	Soubasse	32	30
40	Montre (1–6 from #41)	16	24
41	Soubasse	16	30
42	Flûte ouverte	8	30
43	Bourdon (ext #41)	8	12
44	Flûte	4	30
45	Cor de nuit	2	30
46	Fourniture IV	2-2/3	120
47	Bombarde	16	30
48	Trompette	8	30
49	Clairon	4	30

Couplers

Grand Orgue, Récit, Positif /

Pédale

Récit, Positif / Grand Orgue

Key action and stop action mechanical, 2 ventils

65

SAINT ANTHONY'S CHURCH

1041 Bloor Street West
Canadian Pipe Organ Company Tubular Action Organ, circa 1923

St. Anthony's Church tubular action Canadian Pipe Organ

For anyone intrigued by a mystery, the history of St. Anthony's Church provides no answers as to why an earlier building, whose cornerstone was laid by His Grace Archbishop Fergus Patrick McEvay in 1909 at the corner of Shanley Street and Gladstone Avenue, was never completed.

Construction of the present St. Anthony's Church, located on the south side of Bloor Street just west of Rusholme Road, was blessed by Archbishop Neil McNeil on 24 September 1922. In a document dated 18 July 1923, the architect of the church, Arthur W. Holmes, described the church in the following words: "The architectural character of St. Anthony's Church is Romanesque of circular type built of brick and stone with a steel roof. The interior finish is of oak with oak wainscoting, the floors being of Douglas fir; ceiling with steel trusses and formed with metal lath and plaster with ornamental cornices and ribs. There are two Granite columns dividing the transept from the nave which are arched over."[1]

The plan is essentially the plan used in the early Roman Christian basilica: a long, three-aisled nave, intercepted by a transept and terminated by a semicircular apse over the high altar. The ceiling over this area is crowned by a conch, or half-dome. Small chapels on either side of the main altar echo the shape, but in quarter size, of the main apse.

In the historical antecedent, the two side-aisles were somewhat separated from the central nave by supporting arcades. These arcades were structural necessities, both when the basilica roof was a trabeated structure and later when it became a vaulted form.

At St. Anthony's, the use of steel trusses has permitted the architect to do away with the arcades, which would have obstructed the views of the altar from many positions in the room. What we find, rather, is a central plaster barrel vault which appears to be supported on segments of a lower, wider arch (ribbed, similar to a sexpartite vault) over the side aisles. The transepts have their own high, narrow barrel vaults.

In addition to the arched and vaulted masonry forms, the interiors of Romanesque churches are generally characterized by rich frescos on some or all walls. The most frequently occurring theme is the *Maiestas Christi*, an image which was usually reserved for the conch over the altar. This "Christ the King" is traditionally enclosed in an oval frame known as a mandoria, the symbol of divine glory. This is exactly what we find at St. Anthony's Church. To either side we have symbolism representing the Evangelists Mark and Luke. At the highest point of the half-dome are Matthew and John, with the descending dove of the Holy Spirit. All of this glorious imagery, by an unknown fresco artist, was restored to its original splendour in the late 1990s.

At the opposite end of the room, over the entrance, a substantial gallery accommodates the choir and supports the Canadian Pipe Organ Company organ, below the rose window.

This organ is entirely original and is one of the few remaining examples of tubular pneumatic action in Toronto. In 1967, the leather pouches of the Great and Swell were re-leathered and the organ cleaned. Tuning was discontinued in 1970, when the guitar and drum era started. Maintenance resumed after 1979 and the reservoirs were re-covered in 1988. The organ was cleaned again in 1998, and the pipes and action were re-regulated.

The Canadian Pipe Organ Builders were located in St. Hyacinthe, Quebec. Simon Couture, Casavant historian, writes, "In the 20th century, the Compagnie d'orgues canadiennes/Canadian Pipe Organ Company, founded in St. Hyacinthe in 1910 by two former Casavant employees, J. N. Daudelin and Ludger Madore, was quite active until 1930. As far as I know, this firm built mainly

St. Anthony's Church is a prime example of the rich multi-cultural fabric which can be found in a Toronto parish. Masses are conducted every weekend in English, Portuguese, and Italian.

relatively small tubular organs. The chancel organ at St. Roch Church in Quebec City is in my opinion the best example of this company's work."

There are some interesting features present in the St. Anthony organ. For one, the Pedal Echo Bourdon 16 has a device designed to keep the pipes in tune when the pressure is changed. When the Bourdon 16 is on, long rails rise up to shade the mouths of the pipes and flatten the pitch. When only the Echo Bourdon is on, the rails drop down to sharpen the pitch and compensate for the low pressure. Back at the Casavant shop, the system was to keep the same wind pressures for both stops but to provide a wide windway for the Bourdon and a very narrow windway for the softer Echo Bourdon.

The Great has a "Labial Trumpet." This means the pipes do not have the usual shallots and brass tongues. They are really very hard-blown flue pipes of the Gamba family. The notes are loud enough to play a solo line but there the comparison ends. A loud string sound is not a trumpet tone. Labial reeds were also made by S. R. Warren and Estey.

The placing of five of the Great stops under expression is novel. A similar arrangement was used on the larger S. R. Warren Gallery Organ in St. Andrew's Presbyterian Church, King Street in 1884.

1. *A Vision Shared, the Fresco at St. Anthony's Church*, Fr. Ezio Marchetto, C.S.

Canadian Pipe Organ Company Tubular Action Organ, circa 1923

GREAT ORGAN	FEET	PIPES
(UNENCLOSED STOPS)		
1 Open Diapason	8	65
2 Violin Principal	4	65
3 Labial Trumpet	8	65
(enclosed stops)		
4 Melodia	8	65
5 Doppel Flute	8	65
6 Dolce	8	65
7 Harmonic Flute	4	65
8 Fifteenth	2	61

SWELL ORGAN (ENCLOSED)		
9 Horn Diapason	8	65
10 Night Horn	8	65
11 Viola di Gamba	8	65
12 Viole d'Orchestra	8	65
13 Aeoline	8	65
14 Voix Celeste Ten C	8	53
15 Violes Celestes II (combines #12 with #14)	8	—
16 Concert Flute	4	65
17 Piccolo	2	61
18 Royal Tromba	8	65
19 Orchestral Oboe	8	65
20 Vox Humana	8	65
Tremulant		

PEDAL ORGAN		
21 Double Open Diapason	16	30
22 Bourdon	16	30
23 Echo Bourdon (#22 on lower pressure)	16	—
24 Bass Flute (ext #21)	8	12

COUPLERS
Great, Swell to Pedal 8, 4
Swell to Great 16, 8, 4
Great to Great 16
   (with Open
   Diapason 8 cut-out)
Great 8 off, Great 4
Swell to Swell 16, 8 off, 4

PISTONS (HOLD-SET ADJUSTABLE)

Great & Pedal	1	2	3	Thumb
Swell	1	2	3	Thumb
General	1	2		Toe
Adjuster				
Cancel				

REVERSIBLE PISTONS
Great, Swell to Pedal   Thumb
Swell to Great   Thumb

BALANCED PEDALS
Great expression (mechanical)
Swell expression (mechanical)

Pistons electro-pneumatic,
battery powered

SAINT BASIL'S CHURCH

50 St. Joseph Street
Pre-1919 Tracker Organ
(probably S. R. Warren)
Casavant Opus 800, 1919, Revised 1981

The Casavant Organ of 1919 in St. Basil's R. C. Church.

The graceful plaster arches which now grace the interior of St. Basil's church are not original. They were added in 1922 sealing off forever the additional natural light which used to come into the nave through roof dormers, still visible on the exterior.

As late as 1850 there were only two Roman Catholic churches in Toronto, a city of some 25,000 inhabitants. When Father Armand-Francois-Marie, Comte de Charbonnel, was appointed second Bishop of Toronto, he appealed to the Basilians in Annonay, France, to assist in establishing a third parish, today known as St. Basil's Church.

For their new edifice, to be located north of the town on property known as "Clover Hill," the Basilians selected the Scottish architect, William Hay. Hay had been recruited by the English architect George Gilbert Scott to oversee the construction of his cathedral in St. John's, Newfoundland. He arrived in Toronto in 1852, and in 1855 prepared plans for St. Basil's Church and an adjoining St. Michael's College.

The building, dedicated in 1856, was one hundred feet in length and fifty feet wide (30.4 metres x 15.2 metres). The architecture of the church at this point in history was definitively the Gothic. The design prepared by William Hay is strongly influenced by 13th century English churches and cathedrals, with their pointed arches and lancet windows, and their emphasis on thin linear articulation rather than on mass and volume. Eric Arthur, in his definitive architectural history, *Toronto, No Mean City*, is highly critical of the crudity of the junction between the college and church buildings, given that they were designed by a single architect. A cloister extending southeasterly from the church has unfortunately never been realized. The cloister would have camouflaged this fault in composition.

In 1877 the north wall of the church was extended by 15.2 metres (50 feet), which provided additional space for the sanctuary and included the present set of stained glass windows of St. Michael, St. Basil and St. Charles Boromeo. The stations of the cross also date from the 1877 renovations. In 1886 a further lengthening, this time in the southward direction, provided the organ gallery and narthex.

The sexpartite plaster vaults were constructed in 1922. Previously, the timber construction of the roof was fully exposed and the dormer windows still visible from the outside provided additional daylight.

A hand-written list of the stops in the earlier tracker organ was submitted by

L. E. Morel in 1919. It gives the scales of each stop and the wind pressure which was 3" water manometer. The name of the builder was not stated but was probably S. R. Warren. There is no indication on the letterhead that Morel was at that time an agent for Casavant. The letterhead pictures a wooden organ blower of his own manufacture. As a "Church Organ Tuner and Repairer" he offered "Anything in the Pipe Organ Line – Organs kept in first-Class Order by Yearly Contract. Organ Blowers Supplied, Practically Noiseless. Small Generators for Electric Action, Specialty – Electric Organs – Tubular Organs."

The organist of St. Basil's Church in 1962 was Victor Togni. He was also Professor of Advanced Organ and Improvisation at St. Michael's Cathedral Schola Cantorum in Toronto. His efforts to raise the standard of church music, including organ building, were cut short in 1965 when he was killed in an auto accident. He once stopped this writer during a telephone conversation and identified the church and organ on the record playing in the background.

Program notes for an evening of organ music and Gregorian chant at St. Basil's entitled "Victor Togni at the Great Organ of St. Basil's Church" include an unidentified quotation – "the loft of the great organ is this privileged place where man, half-way as it were between heaven and earth, makes us forget our trivial concerns in order to lead to Him those who are still moved by the pure Beauty of the Lord." Togni's program of Frescobaldi, de Grigny, Tournemire and Langlais would suit well the organ as rebuilt 20 years later – even more with the acoustic enhanced by the clay-tiled floor.

With the surrounding forest of condominium towers largely hidden from view, a visitor can almost succeed in recapturing the "Clover Hill" on which St. Basil's Church was built in 1856.

72

Pre-1919 Tracker Organ
(probably S. R. Warren)

GREAT ORGAN 58 notes
Bourdon	16
Montre	8
Melodia	8
Dulciana TenC	8
Harmonic Flute	8
Principal	4
Fifteenth	2
Mixture	III
Trumpet	8
Clarinet Ten C	8

SWELL ORGAN 58 notes
Open Diapason	8
Stopped Diapason	8
Aeoline	8
Flute	4
Octave	4
Flautina	2
Cornopean	8
Oboe	8
Tremulant	

PEDAL ORGAN 30 notes
Double Open (metal)	16
Bourdon	16

Casavant Opus 800, 1919
Revised 1981

GRAND ORGUE
1	Montre	16	61
2	Montre	8	61
3	Principal	8	61
4	Flute	8	61
5*	Flute harmonique	8	61
6	Cor de chamois	8	61
7*	Prestant	4	61
8*	Flute harmonique	4	61
9*	Doublette	2	61
10†	Cornet (Ten. F)	III	132
11*	Fourniture	III	183
12†	Cymbale	III	183
13	Trompette (new tongues)	8	61
14	Clairon (new tongues)	4	61
	Grand Orgue 4		

RÉCIT (ENCLOSED)
15	Bourdon	16	61
16*	Bourdon	8	61
17	Viole de gambe	8	61
18	Voix céleste	8	61
19	Octave	4	61
20	Flute traversiere	4	61
21	Nazard	2-2/3	61
22	Quarte de nazard	2	61
23	Tierce	1-3/5	61
24	Plein jeu (new 1962)	III	183
25	Cymbale (new 1962)	III	183
26	Basson	8	61
27	Trompette (new tongues)	8	61
28	Hautbois	8	61
29†	Clairon	4	61
	Tremblant		
	Récit 16		
	Récit 4		

POSITIF (ENCLOSED)
30	Contre gambe	16	61
31	Principal	8	61
32	Flute à cheminée	8	61
33	Viole	8	61
34	Viole céleste	8	61
35†	Prestant	4	61
36	Flute ouverte	4	61
37	Flageolet	2	61
38†	Quinte	1-1/3	61
39†	Fourniture	IV	244
40	Cromorne (new tongues)	8	61
41	Chalumeau (new 1962)	4	61
	Tremblant		
	Positif 16		

PÉDALE
42	Resultant	32	—
43	Flute (wood)	16	32
44	Montre (G. O. #1)	16	—
45*	Soubasse	16	32
46	Bourdon (Récit #15)	16	—
47	Contre gambe (Positif #30)	16	—
48	Octave (20 from #1)	8	12
49	Flute (ext. #45)	8	12
50	Bombarde	16	32
51	Basson (Récit #26)	16	—
52	Trompette (ext. #50)	8	12

COUPLERS
Grand Orgue, Récit, Positif à la Pédale 8, 4
Récit, Positif au Grand Orgue 16, 8, 4
Récit au Positif 16, 8, 4

ADJUSTABLE COMBINATIONS
(CAPTURE TYPE)
Grand Orgue	1	2	3	4	5		Thumb
Récit	1	2	3	4	5		Thumb
Positif	1	2	3	4	5		Thumb
Pédale	1	2	3	4	5		Thumb & toe
General	1	2	3	4	5	6	Thumb & toe

General Cancel
Adjuster

Reversible Pistons
Grand Orgue à la Pédale	Thumb and toe
Récit à la Pédale	Thumb
Positif à la Pédale	Thumb
Récit au Grand Orgue	Thumb
Positif au Grand Orgue	Thumb
Récit au Positif	Thumb
Full Organ	Toe

*Warren pipes
†New pipes 1981

1960
A new Casavant console was installed
1962
Gabriel Kney installed new Swell Mixtures and a Chalumeau 4 for the Positif
1981
The organ was cleaned, re-leathered and tonally revised by Alan T. Jackson and Casavant Frères.

ANALYSIS
Revised Organ of 1981

	STOPS	RANKS	PIPES	REAL STOPS
Grand Orgue	14	20	1169	14
Récit	15	19	1159	15
Positif	12	15	915	12
Pédale	11	3	132	3
Totals	52	57	3375	44

73

SAINT CECILIA'S CHURCH

161 Annette Street
Casavant Organ, Opus 598, 1915

St. Cecilia's R. C. Church, the Casavant, tubular pneumatic action organ.

The 'Portative' organ held by St. Cecilia as depicted by the statue above the altar was an instrument carried in procession in the fourteenth and fifteenth century.

St. Cecilia is the patron saint of music. While it would be gratifying to think that a Bishop assigned this name to a parish so that music would be cherished by the faithful, or to acknowledge his own love of music, this was not the case with respect to this church. Between 1890 and March of 1895, when Archbishop John Walsh established St. Cecilia's parish, Sunday mass had been celebrated in a local school already known as St. Cecilia's Catholic School, originally called St. Mary's School. It seemed natural to pass this name on to the church, since there were no other Roman Catholic churches of that name in the city.

This history of the parish relates closely to the heavy immigration which followed the Great Irish Famine of 1840, the construction of the railways, and the development of the West Toronto Junction area at the intersection of three of the early railway lines. Many of the Irish settled in the neighbourhood, which was reported to be "predominantly Presbyterian as were the railway employees," due to the availability of work in the construction, maintenance and operation of these railways.

A wood-frame, formerly Presbyterian church located on the southwest corner of Pacific Avenue and Annette Street was purchased by the parish and served as an interim place of worship. For the alterations to this building the names of architect and builder have been duly recorded: Post & Holmes and Thos. Wright, respectively. There was an organ loft to the west end, and, in all likelihood, an organ.

The designs for the present church were prepared in 1909, and all we know is that they were "based on a recently constructed Catholic Church in Pickering."[1] The church is constructed of red brick on a stone basement. A tower with steeple is placed at the main entrance at the north end of the church. A limited quantity of dressed stone has been used, at the window sills and the pilaster weatherings contrasting with the brick. The church is in a simple Gothic Revival style, and similar to many others constructed in smaller communities in this province at the turn of the last century. While the nave is rectilinear in plan, without columns that would hinder sight-lines, a vaulted plaster ceiling articulates a central nave and two lower ceiling areas along the outside aisles. Even with the current floor finish, which is carpet, the room has a rich and satisfying acoustic.

In 1917, the interior of the church was painted by a famous artist of the time, Mr. P. C. Brown, but tastes change, and over time some of these paintings were covered. In 1957 the son of the original artist, Thomas Brown, was retained to restore many of the decorations, murals and paintings which enrich the church.

The organ at St. Cecilia's Church is one of very few in Toronto built with tubular pneumatic action which has not been converted to electro-pneumatic action.

The change from mechanical action, with every motion visible, to pneumatic action, using invisible changes of air pressure within lead tubes and rails of wood, would have been as difficult for old-time organ tuners in 1900 to understand as it was for old-time tuners in 1950 to understand electronic diode switching. The coupler actions in tubular systems work on the same principle as transistors. If there is air pressure against the tiny leather diaphragm in the coupler switch, the exhausted tube cannot affect the tube running beyond the cell to the chest.

Tubular pneumatic action really works very well when kept in good regulation, but if expert service is not available, cyphers and slow notes can soon cause frustration for the organist, often leading to a request for electrification. Sometimes the old consoles were converted and electric contacts fitted to the old keys and stop knobs. More often, a new console was installed with the advantage of added pistons. Chest magnets were fitted in place of the lead tubing. The magnets are a "horseshoe" type with double coils using low-voltage direct current to lift an iron disc half the size of a dime to open a tiny port. This is all that is needed to drop the pressure in the "key channel" leading to the "primary pneumatic." The "primary pneumatic" moves the "primary valve" which drops the pressure in the main key channel so that any stop connected to the channel may play the chosen note, all of which happens very quickly.

In 1915 a DC generator, belt-run from the blower, would have been been used to operate the magnets. Batteries were not particularly reliable and were used only for back-up power. Many considered tubular pneumatic action more dependable than electro-pneumatic action.

1. St. Cecilia's Parish, 100th Anniversary 1895-1995

(Above) Behind the inevitable foreground of hydro lines, stop lights and newspaper stands, St. Cecilia's R. C. Church.

Casavant Organ, Opus 598, 1915

Great Organ		Feet	Pipes
1	Open Diapason I	8	65
2	Open Diapason II	8	65
3	Melodia	8	65
4	Dulciana	8	65
5	Principal	4	61
6	Harmonic Flute	4	61
7	Fifteenth	2	61
8	Trumpet	8	65

SAINT CLEMENT'S ANGLICAN CHURCH

59 Briar Hill Avenue
Casavant Organ Opus 1289, 1928, new Positif 1965,
new console 1973, organ rebuilt 1995-2000

SWELL ORGAN (ENCLOSED)

9	Bourdon	16	65
10	Open Diapason	8	65
11	Stopped Diapason	8	65
12	Aeoline	8	65
13	Viola di Gamba	8	65
14	Voix Céleste Ten C	8	54
15	Traverse Flute	4	61
16	Piccolo	2	61
17	Dolce Cornet III 2-2/3		183
18	Cornopean	8	61
19	Oboe	8	61
	Tremulant		

PEDAL ORGAN

20	Open Diapason	16	30
21	Bourdon	16	30
22	Gedackt (from #9)	16	—
23	Stopped Flute (ext #21)	8	12

COUPLERS
(TILTING TABLET REGISTERS)
Swell, Great to Pedal 8
Swell to Great 16, 8, 4
Great Super Octave
Swell Sub and Super Octave

ACCESSORIES
3 combination toe levers to Great
4 combination toe levers to Swell
Great to Pedal reversible toe lever
Mechanical Swell expression
   pedal
Balanced crescendo pedal
2' cutouts with Super couplers
16' cutout with Sub couplers

ACTION
Tubular pneumatic key and stop
action
Ventil windchests.

The five-stop Mead Organ in the gallery of St. Clement's Church was installed in St. James Cathedral in 1841, then moved to St. Paul's Bloor Street before the cathedral burned in 1849. The twelve pedal keys are permanently coupled to the manual keys. The organ can be blown using a pump handle or a modern electric blower added in 1965 when the organ was moved and restored.

Given the realities of limited resources and growing congregations, church buildings have often been "works in progress." The evolution of St. Clement's Church, Eglinton from its inception to the present time is a very good case in point. Organs, too, are often the result of several generations of improvements. Casavant Opus 1289 is such an organ.

The forerunner of St. Clement's Church was the Eglinton Mission sponsored by St. John's Church, York Mills, which served North Toronto. The first mission building had suffered the ill effects of gale-force winds early the morning of November 17, 1891. The storm took out the westerly windows, took off its roof, and damaged some walls. The repaired building was opened in February of the following year. In between these two events, the parish was given the name of the third bishop of Rome, St. Clement. This building was sited along today's St. Clement's Avenue with its chancel to the east more or less where the present

chancel is placed. It was a red brick building with round-headed windows and a little belfry. The choir was "supported by the organist seated just inside the door, who was at the mercy of a hand-pumped organ… Later R. J. Lovell donated a two manual tracker organ which had to be hand pumped using a lever at its side. The pumper received $44 a year for this job."[1] The Lovell organ is probably Lye, Opus 144.

In 1900, after the costs of the first building had been paid off, the congregation petitioned for consecration and also asked if they might become independent of St. John's, York Mills. This same year the first phase of a Parish Hall was constructed to the west of the church. Seven years later, construction continued westward with a second hall. While the original church had to be demolished in 1924 in order to allow for the construction of the present chancel, both phases of the original hall continue to serve the congregation to the present day.

The pressures of serving a growing community forced the congregation to consider the construction of a new church, to seat 800, as early as 1913. With the onslaught of World War I, however, attention was focused on the war efforts and it was not until 1921 that

(Opposite) The gallery Trompette-en-chamade at St. Clement's, Eglinton in arranged in the form of a cross and may be unique.

(Above) After being instructed by Vestry to prepare a church design without columns which might obstruct views, architect Forsey Page successfully realized the colonnaded and atmospheric nave that we know today.

(Above, right) The Positif Organ on the left side of the chancel at St. Clement's, Eglinton was built in 1965 in 'the style of the time' with the little pipes on the outside of the chest.

The casework on the right side of the chancel. Installed in 2000, it places the large pipes on the outside and the small pipes behind, also in 'the style of the time'. The pipes are of 70% tin, polished to a high luster and are all speaking pipes of the Great and Pedal Montres. The earlier case built in 1928 combined zinc bass pipes of the Great and Pedal Diapasons with dummy pipes to fill the space.

the Vestry took steps to look into "the erection of a new church or the enlargement of the present edifice."[1] Among the first members of a special committee which was named to study the matter were the architects C. M. Willmot and Major Forsey Page, who were soon named as the architects.

Initial studies centred around enlarging the existing church, but Page, who had recently returned from Europe, had spent every free moment studying its cathedrals and was "firmly committed to the style of architecture he found there."[1]

One of his plans was for an entirely new church in strongly massed, Modern Gothic Style with, apart from a square tower at the entrance, a distinctly horizontal line and Perpendicular Gothic fenestration. In January 1922, the architects were asked by the Building Committee to proceed with final plans; however, at the Vestry level there was no unanimity to take the necessary steps to proceed – for example, the purchase of additional land, or the funds required by the venture.

It was not until 1924, with the mortgage on the present building fully discharged, that the Advisory Board of the church appointed a sub-committee to begin again to discuss plans with Major Page. A motion carried at the same meeting is of interest. The architect was advised that, when preparing sketches, he was to keep in mind that "a building without columns would probably be more generally approved by the congregation than one with columns."[1] Mr. Page was noted to be the one dissenter, and soon brought forth the present design which included rows of columns between the nave and side aisles. In November the architects were instructed to proceed with the drawings and specifications. The Consecration Stone was laid on April 18, 1925.

The design of the new church was described by

J. Bray in an article in *Construction*, February 1926, as being Early English at its best period, the initial years of the 13th century – "a sincere and scholarly expression of the East Anglican Gothic…an accomplished work." The building measures 46 metres (152 feet) in length and 26.8 metres (88 feet) in width at the transepts. It was designed to accommodate a congregation of 700 and a choir of 53. The stone was brought from three quarries to provide a variety of colour and texture. The slate roof also is variegated in colour.

The interior evokes a sense of mystery with its lowered side aisles, terrazzo floor, and richly decorated, dark roof beams. The chancel area, in contrast, is stark. The wall behind the high altar was always intended to be embellished with a carved reredos, in anticipation of which the three lancet windows were placed at a high elevation. For many years a dossal curtain provided a backdrop for the altar, but since 1974 the wall has been bare. If the dossal curtain had never been taken out to be cleaned, it might still be there since no one could have realized what an improvement in sound reflection would result.

When the new church was being built in 1924, plans included a new organ to cost $2,000 "with an electric blower." After three years of discussion it was decided to buy a three-manual Casavant organ with a Great and Swell in the chancel loft. The Choir organ went to the gallery for want of space, but had very limited use. In 1965 it was replaced by an unenclosed Positif which was cantilevered from the East chancel wall. The following year, the space vacated by the Choir organ was taken by the one-manual, 5-stop tracker organ donated by Dr. R. M. Hilary. It had been in his home on Yonge Street in Aurora since 1919. It was originally acquired for St. James' Cathedral in 1842 from Mead of Montreal and

moved after three years to St. Paul's, Bloor Street. In 1872 it was moved to Trinity Church, Aurora. Since there is no name plate on the organ, there is a possibility that it was only moved, not built, by Mead. The organ was restored and the pump handle, feeders and reservoir made to operate. An electric blower was added for regular use. The presence of 12 pedal pull-down keys makes the organ quite useful.

In 1971, organist John Sidgwick organized a festival of music to raise money for a new console. Then in 1988 the first of a series of generous donations from musician Mr. Don Wright and his wife Lillian provided a Trompette en chamade which was mounted in cross form on the gallery wall. This was followed in 1995 with rebuilding of the Swell Organ and in 2000 with rebuilding of the Great and Pedal Organs and the console electrification all in celebration of the work of past rectors.

To complete the scene at St. Clement's, there resides in one corner of organist Tom Fitches' choir rehearsal room the voicing jack built around 1955 in the Eaton shop and used when Fitches reverts to his other vocation as voicer.

ORIGIN, REVISIONS

189? Edward Lye built Opus 144 for the English Church at Eglinton, Ontario.

1924 The new church built.

1928 Casavant Organ Opus 1289 with 3 manuals and 40 stops installed, Great, Swell and Pedal in the chancel and an enclosed Choir Organ in the gallery.

1965 A new Positif Organ of 8 stops installed on the east chancel wall to replace the distant Choir Organ.

1966 A one-manual tracker organ built possibly by

Mead for St. James Cathedral in 1842 was moved from Aurora and installed in the gallery.

1973 A new 3-manual Casavant console installed.

1988 The Trompette-en-chamade installed on the back wall of the gallery.

1995 Swell Organ rebuilt with Pitman action and new and re-voiced pipework.

1999 New chancel casework installed

2000 Great and Pedal divisions rebuilt with Pitman action and new and re-voiced pipework. The console converted to electric stop action control led by Artisan Classic solid state multi-level piston combination action.

1 *Chronicles of St. Clement, Eglinton: 1891-1991*

Casavant Organ Opus 1289, 1928, new Positif 1965, new console 1973, organ rebuilt 1995-2000

GRAND ORGUE

		FEET	PIPES
1	Bourdon (wood)	16	61
2*	Montre	8	61
3*	Bourdon (1-12 wood)	8	61
4*	Prestant	4	61
5*	Flûte	4	61
6*	Grand quinte	2-2/3	61
7*	Doublette	2	61
8*	Fourniture	IV-V	269
9*	Cornet (Ten.C)	IV	196
10*	Trompette	8	61
11*	Voix humaine	8	61
	Tremblant		
12	Trompette-en-chamade	8	61
	(on gallery wall)		

RÉCIT (ENCLOSED)

13	Principal	8	61
14	Stopped Diapason	8	61
15	Viole de gambe	8	61
16	Voix céleste	8	61
17	Octave	4	61
18*	Flûte	4	61
19*	Nazard (Ten C)	2-2/3	49
20	Flautina	2	61
21*	Tierce	1-3/5	61
22*	Plein jeu	IV	244
23*	Bombarde (1-12 L/2)	16	61
24	Trompette	8	61
25	Hautbois	8	61
26*	Clairon	4	61
	Tremblant		

POSITIF (NEW 1965, UNENCLOSED)

27	Bourdon	8	61
28	Prestant	4	61
29	Flûte à fuseau	4	61
30	Flûte	2	61
31	Larigot	1-1/3	61
32	Sifflet	1	61
33	Cymbale	IV	244
34*	Cromorne	8	61
	Tremblant		
35	Trompette-en-chamade (GO)	8	—

PÉDALE

36	Résultante (from#38,#39)	32	—
37	Flûte (wood)	16	32
38	Soubasse (wood)	16	32
39	Bourdon doux (from #1)	16	—
40*	Montre	8	32
41	Bourdon (ext #38)	8	12
42*	Octave	4	32
43*	Contre-bombarde (L/2 ext #44)	32	12
44	Bombarde	16	32
45	Basson (from #23)	16	—
46*	Trompette (ext #44)	8	12
47*	Clairon (ext #44)	4	12

COUPLERS (ROCKING TABLETS)
Grand Orgue,
   Récit, Postif/Pédale   8
Récit/Grand Orgue 16, 8, 4

Positif/Grand Orgue   8
Récit/Positif   8
Récit/Récit 16, 4
Midi/Grand Orgue, Récit, Positif,
Pédale Clochettes (10 bells)

ANALYSIS

	STOPS	RANKS	PIPES	REAL STOPS
Grand Orgue	12	19	1075	12
Récit	14	17	1012	14
Positif	9	11	671	8
Pédale	12	5	208	5
Totals	47	52	2966	39

REVERSIBLE PISTONS
Grand Orgue/Pédale Thumb & toe
Récit, Positif/Pédale   Thumb
Récit, Positif/
   Grand Orgue   Thumb
Tutti   Toe
Clochettes   Toe

ACTION
Originally electro-pneumatic, Ventil chests converted to Pitman and schwimmer winding.

ADJUSTABLE COMBINATIONS
   (electronic, 99 modes)
Grand Orgue

	1	2	3	4	5	6	
Grand Orgue	1	2	3	4			Thumb
Récit	1	2	3	4			Thumb
Positif	1	2	3	4			Thumb
Pédale	1	2	3	4			Thumb
General	1	2	3	4	5	6	Toe
Cancel & Adjuster							Thumb

Transposer, Memory sequencer, Midi to all manuals and pedal. Crescendo on all stops and couplers (programmable 2 modes)

*New pipes 1995, 2000

SAINT JAMES-BOND UNITED CHURCH

1066 Avenue Road
L. E. Morel Organ 1928, Casavant console 1969

 While to a generation of readers the name "James Bond" will bring back images of Agent 007, the name of this church was selected to "hand down to posterity the united names of the two outstanding churches in the earlier life of our city."[1]

When this building was dedicated in October of 1928, it was to serve as a replacement home to a congregation founded in 1834 as Bond Street Congregational Church, becoming Bond Street United at the time of church union in 1925. It is noteworthy that the congregation had a pipe organ at the Bond Street address as early as 1849, and that in 1878 after their original building burned to the ground, they retained the firm of McCaw & Lennox, who had designed St. Paul's Anglican Church, Bloor Street and Casa Loma, to design a large, octagonal Gothic Revival building that was 24 metres (80 feet) by 27 metres (90 feet), seating fourteen hundred worshippers. This building was demolished in 1981, after suffering serious damage in a fire while serving as the Evangel Temple.

The name of the church became St. James-Bond United when, in 1929, St. James Square United Church, which had been St. James Square Presbyterian Church before church union, amalgamated with Bond United. This congregation dated back to 1837 as a "Congregation under the Missionary Presbytery connected with the United Secession Church in Scotland."[1] Successive names including Bay Street United Presbyterian Church, then Gould Street Church, attest to a congregation which made a number of moves before settling on St. James Square in 1878. This area is now part of the Ryerson University campus.

The congregation of St. James Square Presbyterian Church was musically conservative and instrumental music was not condoned until 1881, when a melodeon was used for mid-week services. "In 1884 a pipe organ was installed to be paid for by those who wanted it."[1] By 1911, opposition to organs and instrumental music would seem to have been overcome, since Casavant Frères were contracted to install their Opus 455 in the church. This Casavant organ was moved to St. Cuthbert's Anglican Church, Bayview Avenue in the mid 1950s when the St. James Square Church was demolished.

St. James-Bond United Church on Avenue Road is a considerably smaller building than either of its ancestors. At first glance a viewer would think that the nave and west front, actually facing east, were the work of two different designers. The nave, with its Early English Gothic lancet windows, is approximately 30 metres (100 feet) long and 11 metres (35 feet) wide. A steeply sloped roof is supported on beautifully-detailed raised chord trusses set on rather low walls (3.5 metres). The large balcony over the narthex is, in fact, just below the ends of the trusses. The style of the façade of the church leans more heavily toward the English Perpendicular. The main entrance and a large flat arched window above, at balcony level, are framed on either side by massive brick pilasters, behind which are the twin stairs to the balcony.

There are large stained glass windows in each transept. At the time of construction, these window openings were triple lancets, but when the St. James Square congregation brought from their previous building a large "Good Shepherd" window which had been installed by Luxfer Studios in 1922, the lancet windows of each transept were replaced by one larger opening, similar in size to the window over the main entrance.

Often when established congregations make a move, arrangements are made to have an organ in place for the dedication of the new church building. In this instance the contract for a new, three-manual organ was awarded to L. E. Morel.

L. E. Morel was an employee at Casavant Frères in St Hyacinthe. In 1904 he was sent to Toronto to install the first Casavant organ in the city at the Church of the Redeemer, Bloor at Avenue Road, and was to remain as a salaried agent. Whether he earned his keep in the ensuing few years is not known, but if he was prospect-

ing for sales, the results showed in 1911 when five new Casavant organs were installed in Toronto, including the four-manual organ for Walmer Road Baptist Church. In 1914, six organs arrived, including the very large organ for St. Paul's, Bloor Street. Relations with head office showed signs of deterioration in 1912 as attested by Morel's handwritten letters to the Casavant brothers. When he criticized the firm for making the same mistakes over and over, the reply from Samuel Casavant recalled that it is the nature of men to take the same sin "d'une confession à l'autre!!"

At some point Morel started building organs in Toronto and his ties with Casavant were severed. The Morel workshop is believed to have been on Vine Avenue near the CPR railway, west of Keele Street. He purchased pipes from Gottfried of Erie, Pennsylvania. They were well-made pipes, strong and similar to the pipes Wurlitzer was making for theatre organs. The chest action was electro-pneumatic, Pitman type with the pouchboards built in a manner used by Casavant for their early experiments with Pitman chest building. The organ now in Leaside United Church, built by Casavant for Bridge Street United Church in Belleville in 1914, Opus 588, has the same design. Pitman action was not standard at Casavant until 1930.

When built, the St. James-Bond organ featured double enclosure. The Swell and Choir division each had expression shutters but, in addition, the whole organ was behind another set of shutters affecting the Great, Swell, Choir and Pedal. The idea could well have swayed the organ committee in Morel's direction. The extra shutters were removed some time prior to 1950.

The contract for the new organ must have required completion of the organ by September 9, 1928. Mr. Morel wrote to advise that it would be impossible to finish on time because of the noise and dust generated by other trades. Most builders today stipulate that they have clear possession of the room for a definite number of days or weeks prior to the completion date. Somehow or other, the organ was made ready and it was played on the specified date. The cost of the organ was about $15,000.00.

In 1969 a new Casavant console was donated and installed. Maintenance became simpler and, whether real or psychological, the organ seemed to sound better. One thing Morel did not do well was build a quiet key action. The key action primaries or distributors for all Morel organs retained the unnecessary secondary valves used in the early days of tubular pneumatic organs. In a more modern chest, a single disc of rubber or felt and leather is drawn by a single pneumatic pouch to relieve the pressure in the key channel leading to all the pouches for that particular note. Morel not only used two valves where one would do, but left the action exposed without effective sound covers. The result is a great clatter that can be heard above the tone of all the softer stops. New Casavant distributors have recently been built and installed in the St. James-Bond United organ.

1 *The St. James-Bond Story,* Daniel S. Duff Editor.

L. E. Morel Organ 1928, Casavant console 1969

GREAT ORGAN

#		FEET	PIPES
1	Open Diapason No. 1	8	61
2	Open Diapason No. 2	8	61
3	Tibia	8	61
4	Dulciana	8	61
5	Principal	4	61
6	Fifteenth	2	61
7	Tuba (from #27)	8	—
	Chimes (Choir)		

SWELL ORGAN (ENCLOSED)

#			
8	Bourdon	16	61
9	Open Diapason	8	61
10	Stopped Diapason	8	61
11	Gamba	8	61
12	Voix Celeste Ten C	8	49
13	Aeoline	8	61
14	Traverse Flute	4	61
15	Principal	2	61
16	Mixture	III	183
17	Cornopean	8	61
18	Oboe	8	61
19	Vox Humana	8	61
	Tremulant		

CHOIR ORGAN (ENCLOSED)

#			
20	Dulciana	8	61
21	Rohrflöte	8	61
22	Principal	4	61
23	Waldflöte	2	61
24	Quint	1-1/3	61
25	Clarinet	8	61
26	French Horn	8	61
27	Tuba	8	61
	Tremulant		

PEDAL ORGAN

#			
28	Double Open Diapason (wired from #29, 30)	32	—
29	Open Diapason	16	32
30	Bourdon	16	32
31	Gedackt (from #8)	16	—
32	Bass Flute (ext #30)	8	12
33	Concert Flute (ext #29)	8	12
34	Trombone (ext #27)	16	12
35	Spare knob used for Great Super		
36	Spare knob used for Swell to Great 16		
37	Spare knob used for Swell to Great 4		

COUPLERS

Great, Swell, Choir to Pedal 8
Swell, Choir to Great 8
Swell to Choir 8

COMBINATION PISTONS (CAPTURE TYPE)

Great, Swell, Choir 1-5   Thumb
Pedal, General 1-5 Thumb and Toe
General Cancel
    and Adjuster   Thumb
6 reversible pistons
Balanced Pedals
Swell expression,
    Choir expression
Crescendo

SAINT JAMES' CATHEDRAL

65 Church Street
Casavant Organ Opus 1530, 1936, 1966-7, S.R. Warren 1853,1889
J. W. Walker console 1979

(Opposite) St. James' Cathedral east aisle casework. Tenders for the east and west aisle cases were sent out in 1891. It is not known who carved the cases which are of extraordinary beauty.

F.W. Cumberland's design for St James' Cathedral was partly inspired by the design of Trinity Church, Wall Street, New York. Antecedents include Salisbury Cathedral. The building was constructed of buff brick with stone used only where it had a structural or decorative purpose. The spire was added in 1872-73 at the same time as the Ohio sandstone finials and porches.

St. James' Cathedral is the successor building to the first house of worship to be constructed in the Town of York, later to become Toronto. Construction of the first church began in 1805 under the leadership of the Rev. George Okill Stuart. Given that this was a pioneering community, the intention was to provide for the worship of residents of all denominations.

A second church, this one still Georgian Classical in style but made of stone, was built in 1833. In 1839 the building, along with its organ, was destroyed by fire.

On April 9, 1849 a large area of the commercial core of the town was destroyed by fire. Over its history, Toronto has experienced a number of major fires, and each disaster seemed to leave in its wake an opportunity to put in place an improved framework for the ongoing development of the community. Following the 1849 fire, for example, Town Council enacted new regulations which obliged builders to construct using only solid, first-class materials. The St. Lawrence Market was rebuilt on a grander scale than St. Lawrence Hall, and St. James' Cathedral, the seat of the Anglican Bishop of Toronto (Bishop Strachan at the time), was afforded an opportunity to build a structure more appropriate to its stature.

When, in June 1849, the Vestry advertised an open competition for the design of the new church, no consensus as to the general form of the building had

(Opposite) The rear gallery organ casework in St. James Cathedral was designed by Frederick Cumberland and built by Jacques & Hay of Toronto. It first screened the Warren Organ of 1853 but was large enough to hide the double-decked expression box of the 1936 Casavant Organ plus the chest of Trumpet pipes, 16', 8' and 4' placed on top in 1966.

(Left, inset) The chancel cases were built in 1916 with pipes which extended far above the top line of the woodwork. The ugly feature was corrected in 1967 by removing the extra length from the tops of the pipes.

been reached. There were those who wanted to rebuild an unostentatious parish church and others who felt that the new plan should be reoriented from that of the destroyed church so that the main doors would properly face west.

F. W. Cumberland, a local architect, won the competition. Working first with Thomas Ridout Jr. and later with William G. Storm, Cumberland redesigned as required by a Vestry which kept changing its mind. Following the competition he was first asked to produce a design which might fit the foundations of the old church. This alternate design was accepted, but then a decision was made to place the new building in the centre of the churchyard in spite of the efforts to reuse the foundations. The first masonry was laid in September 1850.

Although all the designs of the three previous St. James' Churches were a response to the prevailing Georgian, classical tastes of the times, by the mid-nineteenth century the Gothic style had become recognized as the appropriate one for church buildings. Cumberland's design was partly inspired by the design of the American architect, Richard Upjohn, for Trinity Church, Wall Street, New York. This church had been built between 1840 and 1846 and was the most lavish and best-publicized church in North America at the time. Antecedents include a number of important English medieval churches, the 12th-century Salisbury Cathedral being one of the most noteworthy. Due to the high cost of stone, the building was constructed of "white" (buff) brick with stone used only where it had a structural or decorative purpose.

Tight finances also kept the Vestry from adding the tower until over fifteen years later, when Henry Langley oversaw the completion of the tower in 1866, basically following Cumberland's designs. The spire was added in 1872-73 at the same time as the Ohio sandstone finials and porches.

At 306 feet, the tower with its spire is the tallest church steeple in Canada and the second tallest in North America after New York's St. Patrick's Cathedral. In all likelihood it would have crowned the Toronto skyline until the construction of the Royal York Hotel and the Canadian Bank of Commerce, both in 1929. The tower houses two sets of bells. At the highest level is a chime of ten fixed bells, last enlarged in 1928. In 1996, funded by many business leaders in the surrounding commercial district, a ring of twelve bells was installed in a lower belfry. This is the only ring of twelve bells in North America. Many of the bells for this set came from St. James' Church, Jamaica Road, London for which they were cast by Mears & Stainbank in 1828.

Conservative members of the congregation were pleased to find that the floor plan duplicated the wide nave, aisles and south tower location of the previous building. Pew holders found that they could remain in their accustomed locations. A heavily timbered roof structure is a dramatic feature of the interior.

The additional balcony capacity provided by Cumberland was removed in 1888 under the supervision of the architect Frank Darling. This change made the room infinitely more spacious and, very likely, more reverberant.

While Cumberland's chancel represented an increased area from that of the previous church, and, with its polygon shape, was more interesting, it is an element in the overall visual composition which could have used more depth. Nevertheless in this tight area all the requirements of a cathedral seem to have been met – the area contains the altar, the bishop's throne, choir and canon stalls, even Bishop Strachan's tomb, while permitting the choir area to be part of the same acoustical space as the nave.

The contract to build an organ for the cathedral in 1936 in the depths of the Great Depression would have been a welcome turn of events. Before the crash of October 1929, the Casavant Brothers were building between 50 and 60 organs a year. This dropped to about 15 in 1934 and 19 in 1936. The instruments were being built by the supervisors and foremen and it is unlikely that there was much, if any, unskilled help.

There was concern during the design process that there was not enough opening for the sound and in particular, sound for the organist at the head of the chancel. During the installation in November 1936, Mr. Stoot, the Technical Director, wrote back to the shop saying, "The work at St. James' Cathedral is progressing satisfactorily but the main organ has lost about 50% of its volume by being enclosed between stone walls." Much consideration was given to changing the situation when discussion began with organist Mr. Hurrle and Mr. Phelps, Tonal Director for Casavant Frères, in 1965. The first year of the project was partly experimental involving re-spacing of the front pipes by removing pipes that were not speaking pipes and by filling the walls and ceilings of the organ chamber with sealer. The second year saw the replacement of ranks that would not respond to re-voicing and the addition of new pipes and chests. We think that Mr. Stoot would have been pleased with the final result.

St. James' Cathedral is one of the few buildings in Toronto which can maintain a reverberant, musically pleasing surround of sound when full of people. It is lofty enough, is free of side galleries and has wide aisles clear of carpet. Stops in the Antiphonal Organ can be

90

mixed with those at the front and it is often difficult to identify the source of the sound. The exception is the Trompeta Real which would not be doing its job if it did not make its presence known.

Origins, revisions

1833 a second church was built, the music accompanied by instruments.

1838 27-stop Gray & Davidson of London organ installed, cost £1,200.

1839 church and organ of 1838 burned.

1840 5-stop Mead Organ from Montreal installed in the third church but was too small.

1845 Mead Organ sold to St. Paul's Church; Organ replaced by a May and Son Organ from Adelphi Terrace, London.

1849 church burned and the May and Son organ sent a shower of hot lead down to the floor.

1853 present cathedral built and £1,569 was paid to S. R. Warren for a new organ which was ready for trial on June 2, 1853. It was a 3-manual tracker organ of 37 stops built in the gallery. The casework was designed by the architect, Frederick Cumberland, and was built by Jacques & Hay of Toronto at a cost of £303.10.0. This casework remains today.

1878 The organ was overhauled at a cost of $3,274.55 and a water motor installed to blow the organ.

1888 S.R. Warren & Sons signed a contract for $10,000 to rebuild the organ in the front of the cathedral, divided on two sides with the console on the east side and the new hydraulic blower was placed behind in what had been a vestry. The side galleries were removed and large openings made in the front walls either side.

1889 Tenders for the two aisle cases went out in 1891 but they were not immediately installed.

1906 a Warren Echo Organ was donated by Mrs. Gooderham and installed in the gallery after 8 years of discussion. It cost $1,400.

1916 the two chancel cases were installed.

1921 Organist Dr. Ham complained of action trouble in Echo and Pedal divisions.

1936 Casavant Frères rebuilt the entire organ with new Pitman chests, 4-manual console, enclosed Echo organ, Opus 1530 with 79 stops, pipes largely from organs of the previous Warren organs. The console was located on the Gospel side near the communion rail.

1966 first phase of tonal renovation designed by organist Norman Hurrle and Lawrence Phelps, Tonal Director of Casavant Frères. The organ was cleaned, Swell, Choir and Echo fitted with schwimmer wind, dummy façade pipes removed from cases, Choir Tubas 16', 8', 4' pipes and chest moved to gallery, reeds re-voiced by Casavant, console refurbished, flues re-voiced on location mainly by Thomas Fitches working on a voicing jack installed in the narthex.

1967 a second contract with Alan T. Jackson to complete tonal revisions including 34 ranks of new Casavant pipes.

1976 new Spanish Trumpet installed in gallery by L.I. Phelps & Associates.

1979 new 4-manual, movable console installed by J. W. Walker and Sons.

1984 29 treble pipes added to the Pedal Lieblich Gedeckt 16 for the Choir manual 16 by Jerroll Adams of Michigan.

2000-1 new Pedal Contra Basson 32' wooden resonators, 1 –12 being 1/2 length, the remainder full length, by P&S Organ Supply installed by Andrew Mead, a Pedal flute 4' and a Zimbelstern also by Andrew Mead; a new movable platform for the console by Henk Berentschot (Durham Mfg. Co. of Whitby).

Casavant Organ Opus 1530, 1936, 1966-7, S. R. Warren 1853, 1889 J. W. Walker console 1979

GREAT ORGAN w.p. 3-1/2"

		FEET	PIPES
1	Double Open Diapason	16	68
2	Open Diapason I	8	68
3	Open Diapason II	8	68
4	Open Diapason III	8	68
5	Doppelflöte	8	68
6	Octave	4	68
7	Viola	4	68
8*	Nachthorn	4	68
9	Twelfth	2-2/3	61
10	Fifteenth	2	61
11*	Blockflöte	2	61
12	Mixture III	1-1/3	183
13	Mixture II	1/2	122
14*	Cornet V Ten F	8	220
15†	Trompeta Real (Aux)	8	—

SWELL ORGAN (ENCLOSED) w.p. 4"

16	Open Diapason	8	68
17	Stopped Diapason	8	68
18	Viola da Gamba	8	68
19	Quintadena	8	68
20	Aeoline	8	68
21	Voix Céleste	8	68
22*	Octave	4	68
23*	Spillflöte	4	68
24*	Principal	2	61
25	Quinte	1 1/3	61
26*	Plein Jeu V	2	305
27	Klein Mixture III	1	183
28	Posaune	16	68
29	Contra Fagotto	16	68
30	Cornopean	8	68
31	Oboe	8	68
32	Clairon	4	68
	Tremulant		

CHOIR ORGAN (ENCLOSED) w.p. 4"

33	Lieblich Gedackt	16	61
34	Open Diapason	8	68
35*	Gedackt	8	68
36	Principal	4	68
37*	Spizflöte	4	68
38*	Nazard	2-2/3	61
39*	Waldflöte	2	61
40*	Tierce	1-3/5	61
41*	Scharff IV	1/2	244
42	Krummhorn	8	68
	Tremulant		
43†	Double Trumpet (Aux)	16	—
44†	Trumpet (Aux)	8	—
45†	Clairon (Aux)	4	—
46†	Trompeta Real (Aux)	8	—

AUXILIARY ORGAN (EXPRESSIVE) w.p. 3-5/8", reeds 5-3/4"

47	Open Diapason	8	68
48	Gedackt	8	68
49	Spitzflöte	8	68
50	Spitzflöte Céleste Ten C	8	56
51	Principal	4	68
52	Twelfth	2-2/3	61
53	Fifteenth	2	61
54*	Mixture II	2/3	122
55†	Double Trumpet	16	68
56†	Trumpet	8	68
57	Basset Horn	8	68
58	Vox Humana	8	68
59†	Clairon	4	68
60†	Trompeta Real	8	61
	Tremulant		

AUXILIARY PEDAL

61	Open Diapason	16	32
62	Bourdon	16	32

PEDAL ORGAN

63	Sub Bourdon	32	32
64	Open Diapason	16	32
65	Principal (from #1)	16	—
66	Bourdon	16	32
67	Lieblich Gedackt (from #33)	16	—
68*	Principal	8	32
69	Pommer	8	32
70*	Fifteenth	4	32
71	Flute	4	32
72*	Nachthorn	2	32
73*	Mixture V	2-2/3	160
74	Contra Basson (1-12 L/2)	32	32
75	Posaune	16	32
76	Fagotto (from #29)	16	—
77	Trumpet (ext #75)	8	12
78	Fagot (from #29)	8	—
79	Krummhorn (from #42)	4	—
80	Trompeta Real (from #60)	8	—

ANALYSIS

	STOPS	RANKS	PIPES	REAL STOPS
Great	15	21	1252	14
Swell	17	23	1494	17
Choir	14	13	828	10
Aux.	16	17	1037	16
Pedal	18	15	492	11
Totals	80	89	5,103	68

COUPLERS & ACCESSORIES

Great, Swell, Choir, Aux. to Pedal 8, 4
Swell, Choir, Aux. to Great 16, 8, 4
Swell, Aux, to Choir 16, 8, 4
Choir, Aux. to Swell 8
Swell, Choir, Aux. Sub, Super, 8 off
Great Super, 8 off
Pedal 8 off
Great & Pedal Piston Coupler
All Shutters to Swell Pedal
Swell, Choir, Nave shutters on/off
Zimbelstern

ADJUSTABLE COMBINATION PISTONS

8 Great thumb pistons
8 Swell thumb pistons
8 Choir thumb pistons
8 Aux. thumb pistons
8 Pedal toe pistons
12 General thumb and toe pistons
Divisional stop and coupler cancel all manuals and pedal
Octave Coupler Cancel
General Cancel

REVERSIBLE PISTONS

All 8' manual couplers. Thumb
All 8' Pedal Couplers, thumb and toe
Sub Bourdon 32' thumb and toe
Contra Basson 32' thumb and toe
Full Organ thumb and toe

*new pipes 1967
†reeds unenclosed

SAINT JOHN'S CHURCH, WEST TORONTO

288 Humberside Avenue
C. Franklin Legge, Opus 211, 1947
Rebuild including new Choir Division by David Legge, 1966
Casavant Console Opus 1315 (1929) installed by Alan Jackson & Company, 2000

Constructed on a low site in a neighborhood of hills and valleys, St. John's Church, West Toronto is often overlooked by passers by, in spite of a nave placed a full floor above grade, and its substantial bell tower.

(Overleaf) St. John's Anglican, West Toronto. The C. Franklin Legge Organ dates from 1947, about the time that Franklin Legge died as the result of an auto accident. Later additions such as the towers of Open Metal 16' pipes and the exposed Great and Choir chests were by David Legge, Franklin's son.

St. John's Church, West Toronto, located on Humberside Avenue at Quebec Avenue, is the parish's third building. The congregation was formed in 1879, and by 1881 had settled into a simple wood-frame church at the corner of Dundas Street West and St. John's Road in the West Junction area of Toronto. By 1890, the congregation had the wherewithal to have architects Strickland and Symmons produce a design for a red-brick church to seat 350, adjacent to the first building which then became the church hall.

It soon became apparent that, with new residential development south of Dundas Street West, this first site was no longer geographically the centre of the parish, and there were discussions related to the purchase of the current property and the moving and reconstruction of the church. One letter dated November 8, 1918 makes a recommendation to Mr. G. P. Reid, Secretary-Treasurer of the Synod Office, "that the present Church be taken down and removed to the new site, and that the new Church be built of the material of the present Church, and on the lines of the completed Church as per plans in the Vestry of the existing Church. This with a view to the continuance of the historical connection of the present building...."

While construction of the current building did proceed in 1923 on the current site, the "plans" of which the letter spoke seem no longer to exist; there seems to be no architect of record, and there is no evidence that materials from the previous church were worked into the new building. The church is a simple red rug brick building on a Credit Valley stone basement. Stylistically it is inspired by early English Gothic and has a strong resemblance to the St. John's Road church. Perhaps due to site constraints, the emphasis on the plan is on width and height, not on length. A first rendering which appears in the 1922 Annual Vestry Report shows a building not as wide: it has two pairs of main doors rather than three below a double rather than a triple window.

However, the corner tower, with its eight merlons rising from its parapet, remained unchanged from the first scheme to the completed church, even though it was always referred to as being an "option in the architect's plans." By 1924 a set of

ten bells cast by Gillett and Johnston, Croydon, England had been installed, the focus of a fund-raising effort independent from the funds required to construct the church. This represented a costly enhancement. Construction of the church was reported to have cost $82,515.68; the bells cost an additional $10,668.74.

The Ascension Window located above the high altar is the only stained glass window which dates from the dedication of the church. It was installed by Luxfer Studios, and is a memorial to the 39 men of the Parish who had lost their lives in the Great War of 1914-1919.

The first reference to a pipe organ in the Vestry records dates from 1909 when a Vestry report entry states "balance owing on the pipe organ is due, and the church from which the organ was purchased is pressing for the amount of $450.00." This was a hand-pumped organ, built by the Lye Organ Co., Toronto. In 1910 Vestry voted that $200.00 be used to provide a powered blower for this organ. In 1923, upon completion of the new church on Humberside Avenue and sale of the church building located on the St. John's Sideroad, this organ was moved to the new sanctuary.

The present organ, constructed by C. Franklin Legge, organ builder and member of the Parish, was a major rebuild of the previous organ. Although Legge had proposed to install a new organ of "straight" design, this was rejected because it would cost too much. The rebuild is reported to have used "old pipes and casework but new working parts."

The specification was incrementally expanded over the years by David Legge, the son of Franklin. In 1959 the organ was cleaned and the current swell shutters installed. A Melodia built by Casavant was added to the Great Organ and an Oboe from Saskatoon (builder unknown) was added to the Swell. Additions were also made to the strings of the Great and Swell.

The Deagan Chimes were added in 1961, and in 1962 a new Great Chest was extended into the Chancel. This chest carried a number of new ranks supplied by Heyhusan of Holland (Twelfth, Superoctave and Mixture).

The Choir division was added by David Legge in 1966 in memory of Percy Wicker MacDonald, composer and organist of the church for a period of forty years. An existing, re-voiced clarinet was moved to this division and the division was reported to include the three other stops listed in the specification. The whereabouts of the 2' Flautino is not presently known.

In 1981 the Pedal Open Metal 16' was added. It came from a Breckels and Matthews organ that was being removed from Parkdale United Church (c. 1895), before the demolition of that distinguished church building.

The origin of the Pedal Trombone stop, which is an extension of the Great Trumpet, is also remarkable. These twelve pipes with their full-length resonators were first built for the organ of Erskine Presbyterian Church, now the Erskine and American United Church, on Sherbrooke Avenue in Montreal. This instrument was built in 1893 by the firm of S. R. Warren and Son of Toronto, but in all likelihood the 16' reed pipes date from Casavant's work on the instrument in 1909. While no markings have been found on the pipes as to their manufacture, they resemble closely the work of the Cavaillé-Coll firm of Paris and might have been crafted by that firm for Casavant, or might have been built by Casavant following designs imported by Casavant Frères from France.

On the subject of design origins, it should be pointed out that the original Pitman chests (Swell and original portion of the Great) were built by C. Franklin

Legge's St. Hyacinthe branch factory and are identical to Casavant chests being built at the time – likely by tradesmen who had been trained within the Casavant organization.

In 1996 Alan Jackson & Co. was retained to remove all pipework from the organ chamber in order to facilitate a rebuilding of the chamber. The pipework was cleaned at this time.

In October of 2000, the church purchased a used three-manual Casavant console, which had been built for Darke Hall of Regina College in 1929. Regina College became the University of Regina, and when there were plans to demolish the university concert hall in the early 1990s the organ was sold in its entirety to St. Andrew's Presbyterian Church of Sarnia. Since the console was not required for their organ enlargement project, it was sold to St. John's Church, West Toronto. The console was installed by Alan Jackson & Co. in a location closer to the nave altar.

C. Franklin Legge, Op. 211, 1947 Rebuild including new Choir Division by David Legge, 1966 Casavant Console Opus 1315 (1929) installed by Alan Jackson & Company, 2000

GREAT ORGAN	FEET	PIPES
1 Bourdon	16 (prep)	
2 Diapason	8	61
3 Melodia	8	61
4 Dulciana	8	61
5 Principal	4	61
6 Waldflote	4	61
7 Twelfth	2-2/3	61
8 Superoctave	2	61
9 Mixture III	1-1/3	183
Trumpet (from #25)	16	—
Trumpet (from #25)	8	—
Trumpet (from #25)	4	—
(trumpets available on		
couplers from Echo)		
Great to Great 16, 4 couplers		

SWELL ORGAN (ENCLOSED)		
10 Geigen Principal	8	61
11 Stopped Diapason	8	61
12 Viol de Gamba	8	61
13 Voix céleste GG	8	54
14 Octave	4 (prep.)	
15 Flauto Traverso	4	61
16 Picolo	2	61
17 Fagot	16 (prep)	
18 Cornopean	8	61
19 Oboe	4	61
Tremulant		
Swell to Swell 16, 4 couplers		

CHOIR ORGAN		
20 Hohlflote	8	61
21 Leiblich Principal	4	61
22 Flautino	2 (prep)	
23 Clarinet	8	61
24 Chimes 21 tubes		
Tremulant		
Choir to Choir 16, 4 couplers		

ECHO ORGAN		
25 Trumpet		
(on Gt. chest)	8	61
26 through 31		
(prepared for on console)		

PEDAL ORGAN		
32 Resultant (from #34)	32	—
33 Open Diapason		
(ext. #38)	16	12
34 Bourdon	16	32
35 Gedackt (from #34)	16	—
37 Stopped Flute		
(ext. #34)	8	12
38 Gemshorn		
(from #21)	8	12
39 Trombone (from #25)	16	12
40 Trumpet (from #25)	8	—
41 Clairon (from #25)	4	—

Total of 1229 pipes
29 stops
24 ranks

COUPLERS
Great, Swell, Choir,
   Echo to Pedal 8
Swell to Pedal 4
Swell, Choir,
   Echo to Great 16, 8, 4
Echo to Great Off
Swell to Choir 16, 8, 4
Echo to Choir 8

ADJUSTABLE COMBINATIONS
   (CAPTURE TYPE)

Great	1	2	3	Thumb
Swell	1	2	3	Thumb
Choir	1	2	3	Thumb
Echo	1	2	3	Thumb
Pedal	1	2	3	Thumb
General	1	2	3	Toe

General Cancel
Adjuster

REVERSIBLE PISTONS
Great to Pedal	Thumb and toe
Swell to Pedal	Thumb
Choir to Pedal	Thumb
Echo to Pedal	Thumb
Full Organ	Toe

Balanced Pedals
Swell expression pedal
(Two additional expression
   pedals not utilized)
Crescendo

SAINT JOHN'S, YORK MILLS

19 Don Ridge Drive
Casavant Organ Opus 1969, 1949

The Parish of St. John's, York Mills was the second to be established in what is today the Anglican Diocese of Toronto. Although there were other churches before this that had acquired a resident priest, St. John's was established but relied on missionaries and travelling priests for its clergy. The cornerstone for St. John's, York Mills was laid on May 30, 1843. On July 20 of the same year the cornerstone of Trinity Episcopal Church, King Street was laid. Trinity, now called 'Little Trinity' opened on February 14, 1844 and St. John's, York Mills opened on May 30, 1844. Both claim to have the oldest building. The architect of the 1844 church was John George Howard.

Howard, who held the name of John Corby until his emigration to Upper Canada, came from Hertfordshire. His voyage was a very eventful one, and he had the misfortune of arriving during Toronto's Asiatic Cholera plague of 1832. Although he originally intended to settle in Goderich, he decided upon arrival that York held better prospects for his future. Lieutenant Governor Sir John Colborne soon offered Howard the position of drawing master at Upper Canada College, which provided an ideal introduction to those in the community requiring the services of an architect.

Howard was involved in the design of a number of churches including St. John's Church, Peterborough (1838), the Church of the Holy Trinity, Chippawa and the first St. Paul's Anglican Church in Yorkville (1841).

(*Previous page*) *St. John's, York Mills is one of three, square-ended hall churches designed by the architect John Howard. The churches of Christ Church, Holland Landing, and Christ Church, Tyendenaga are identical plan and differ only in detail. All have three-stage bell towers similar to that of St. John's.*

The cornerstone for St. John's, York Mills, was laid on May 30, 1843. On July 20 of the same year the cornerstone of Trinity Episcopal Church, King Street was laid. Trinity, now called 'Little Trinity' opened on February 14, 1849 and St. John's, York Mills opened on May 30, 1844. Both claim to have the oldest building.

The English barrel organ in the gallery of St. John's, York Mills, still playable, has been there since 1847. There are five stops and no keyboard. Turning a crank pumps the wind needed for the pipes and also turns the barrel.

St. John's, York Mills is his last church design. While Howard was preparing drawings for St. John's (drawings which the church still has today) he was named City Surveyor by the City of Toronto. By 1855 he was virtually retired from practice and living at Colborne Lodge in High Park, his property of 165 acres which was later bequeathed to the City. Today the park has been augmented by municipal acquisitions of 406 acres.

The design which John Howard prepared for St. John's, York Mills' second building is in a pointed Gothic style in buttressed brick, with the corner buttresses angled. A tower over the main entrance is in three stages, with bracketed set-offs culminating in a battlemented crown. A bed of blue clay was discovered nearby from which it was possible to make an excellent "white" (actually a cream colour) burnt brick in place of the ordinary red burnt brick originally planned. The interior was simple, and many of the fittings from the earlier frame building were re-used.

The crank and one of the three barrels in place. The barrels are fitted with staples and pins to operate the stickers and valves which sound the pipes. Each barrel will play ten different hymn tunes.

How often it is that the determination of one or two persons results in the arrival of a new organ. For St. John's in 1846, a Miss Thorne started to collect money for a barrel organ "beginning with the Bishop who subscribed a Pound." Thus "When Col. Thorne left for England in the Spring of 1847 he was able to take with him fifty Pounds toward the cost of the organ."[1] Col. Thorne, Churchwarden, was joined in London by the Second Warden, Joseph Beckett, and they proceeded to the firm of T. C. Bates "where they found an establishment that offered finger organs, pianofortes, seraphines (portable organs), and a whole series of 'Sacred Barrel Organs' – They chose Number 6 as advertised in the literature that accompanied the organ. In the invoice it is described as 'Church Barrel Organ in Solid Oak, Gothic Case, 8ft.6 by 4ft.1 Gilt front on a pedestal; five stops; open diapason, stpt do., Double do., Principal and fifteenth, and one barrel, ten tunes, to order - £40' Two extra barrels were ordered so that the organ had a repertoire of thirty tunes."[1] The organ arrived in September of the same year. There was some damage in shipment which was repaired for £6. 10. 0 by John Thomas, the builder of the first organ in Holy Trinity Church in 1849. Prior to the arrival of the organ, the choir had sung with the aid of a tuning fork. They now had a choice of thirty hymn tunes and the sound of five ranks of pipes with which to sing.

It is understandable that after ten or fifteen years a congregation could get tired of the same thirty tunes as well as the rigid tempo of the music, as the verger turned the crank of the "hand organ." This allowed neither the dragging of the lines nor the inspiration of the moment for an accelerando or ritardando.

Ten years later a special Vestry Meeting was called "to consider the propriety of purchasing in exchange for our (St. John's) organ, a finger organ offered on favourable and advantageous terms."[1] The meeting was adjourned for lack of attendance, and as a result the barrel organ was saved to this day. For many years the barrel organ was played just before the processional hymn. It is still played several times a year. An overhaul of the organ was carried out in the early 1960s by Mr. Leonard Downey and paid for by the Women's Guild.

Pietro Yon, organist of St. Patrick's Cathedral, New York City, expressed the limitations of a barrel organ in his composition *The Primitive Organ*. After hearing a barrel organ in a museum, he imitated musically its monotonous gyrations which suddenly halt after a seemingly interminable period.

The choir and congregation at St. John's began to wish for a "finger organ" (an organ with a key board). Fundraising for a finger organ began in earnest in 1859. However, since it was on the heels of recessionary times in York Mills, the desired result was not achieved until 1864, during the brief incumbency of the Rev. Thomas Tempest Robarts, grandfather of John P. Robarts, former Premier of Ontario. This first finger organ was probably a melodeon or a reed organ.

Archival records indicate that a further Organ Fund was set up in 1879. In 1889 a chancel was introduced with choir stalls (formerly located in the gallery) and another organ was purchased – again, not a pipe organ. To this day, foot-pumped reed organs are common in little country churches. Without carpeting and with a lively acoustic, a reed organ would have been adequate in the simple, rectangular room.

Finally in 1928 the first pipe organ was purchased. It cost $1,900 and was a two-manual-and-pedal Breckels and Matthews organ brought from St. John's Presbyterian Church, Broadview Avenue. In order to accommodate this instrument, a small addition was built to the east of the church to serve as a chamber. Breckels and Matthews also built the organs for St. Mary Magdalene's Church and for St. Stanislas Roman Catholic Church, Denison Avenue. Both organs had electro-

pneumatic action but also had windchests which were difficult to repair.

The pipes of the Breckels and Matthews organ were used to build the Casavant Organ of 1949. This organ was first considered in 1945 at a time when the 300 families in the parish were attending a church that could not seat more than 250 people. The solution was to enlarge the church by removing the east wall, adding transepts and a new chancel area. Work began in the spring of 1948, and it is reported that more than 700 people attended the Dedication service in October of 1949.

Funds for the new Casavant Organ of 1949 were raised by the Women's Guild. When the time came to rebuild the organ in 1969, the final event of the parish's 150th anniversary celebrations, the cost was again carried by the Anglican Church Women.

ORIGINS, REVISIONS

1844 new stone church built.

1847 English barrel organ installed, crank operated.

1864 finger organ installed.

1889 new organ installed.

1928 used Breckels and Matthews organ from St. John's Presbyterian Church, Broadview Avenue installed.

1949 Casavant Organ Opus 1969 installed, 27 stops, pipes from old organ with 13 ranks of new pipes.

1968 organ tonally revised, 16 ranks of new Casavant pipes.

1994 console converted to electric drawknobs with Artisan Classic electronic combinations, new blowers installed.

1 *150 Years at St. John's York Mills,* M. Audrey Graham.

Casavant Organ Opus 1969, 1949

GREAT ORGAN		FEET	PIPES
1*	Pommer	16	61
2*	Prinzipal	8	61
3*	Bordun	8	61
4*	Erzahler	8	61
5*	Oktav	4	61
6*	Spitzflote	4	61
7*	Quint	2-2/3	61
8*	Superoktav	2	61
9*	Mixtur IV	1-1/3	244
10	Trompet (prepared in console)		

Great to Great 4 coupler

SWELL ORGAN (EXPRESSIVE)			
11†	Prinzipal	8	68
12†	Holzgedackt	8	68
13†	Viol de Gamba	8	68
14†	Voix celeste GG	8	61
15†	Prinzipal	4	61
16†	Rohrflote	4	61
17	Nazat	2-2/3	61
18	Oktav	2	61
19	Waldflote	2	61
20	Terz	1-3/5	61
21*	Mixtur IV	1	244
22	Fagot (full length)	16	68
23*	Trompette	8	68
24	Oboe	8	68

Tremulant
Swell to Swell16 coupler
Swell to Swell4 coupler

PEDAL ORGAN			
25	Resultant (from#27&#28)	32	—
26	Open Bass	16	32
27†	Bordun	16	32
28	Gedackt (from #1)	16	—
29†	Prinzipal	8	32
30†	Stopped flute (ext. #27)	8	12
31†	Oktav (ext. #29)	4	12
32	Fagot (from #22)	16	—

COUPLERS
Great, Swell to Pedal 8, 4
Swell to Great 16, 8, 4

ADJUSTABLE COMBINATIONS
(Artisan Classic electronic
combination system 25 levels)

Great	1 2 3 4		Thumb
Swell	1 2 3 4		Thumb
Pedal	1 2 3		Thumb
General	1 2 3 4 5 6 7 8		Toe

General Cancel
Adjuster

REVERSIBLE PISTONS
Great to Pedal   Thumb and toe
Swell to Great   Toe
Full Organ   Toe

BALANCED PEDALS
Chancel Side Swell
    expression pedal
Nave Side Swell expression pedal
Crescendo programmable

*   new pipes 1968
†   Old Breckels and Matthews
      pipes

SAINT LUKE'S UNITED CHURCH

353 Sherbourne Street
Casavant Organ Opus 1356, 1929

In 1871, Elm Street Methodist Church decided to extend its influence into the growing northeast part of the city by establishing a new congregation. Once a site was found, an architect had to be selected. Henry Langley was reported to have been too busy to take on the project, so the group reluctantly appointed Messrs. Smith and Gemmell. The new church, which officially opened in March of 1872, was a plain brick building of Gothic design measuring 16.4 m (54 feet) by 22.8 m (75 feet) plus a porch.

By 1876 the church had grown to the point where it had to be enlarged to accommodate the increase in membership. For this project Langley, Langley and Burke were available and the building was extended to the east by 8 m (26 feet). At this time the original name, Carlton Wesleyan Methodist Church, was changed to Sherbourne Wesleyan Methodist Church so as not to be confused with the nearby Carlton Primitive Methodist Church.

Congregational growth continued to the point that even the enlarged building was inadequate and in 1886 a decision was made to build anew on the same site. It is noteworthy that the church had become a "nesting ground" of wealthy Methodists, to the point where it was dubbed the "Church of the Methodist Millionaires."[1] Again, Henry Langley became involved as the architect of the new church building. Work proceeded almost concurrently with his work on a second Methodist Church – Trinity Methodist, today Trinity-St.

Paul's United Church, at Bloor and Robert Streets.

It was about this time that the firm began to adopt the Richardson Romanesque Style for its more adventurous church clients. Constructed of grey Credit Valley sandstone with dressings of brown sandstone from the same quarry, the completed building was regarded as the "handsomest in central Toronto" at the turn of the century. On the towers, the two colours of stone were used to create a checkerboard effect. The porch and south wing were added in 1960 and, unfortunately, they compromise the compositional integrity of the original building.

Inside, the church was more unusual. The overall feeling was one of being in an opera house, not a church. The seating for 1500 worshippers included long rows of elegant upholstered chairs and there was a large quantity of rich, dark woodwork. It was reported that "the architecture and decorations of the church are rich and soft in tone, and irreproachable in taste."[1]

After the time of church union, a desire to modernize the church building and to make it more suitable for community activities resulted in a much more austere building. Renovations were conducted in 1929, and in 1930 the current organ was installed behind a Moorish-looking plaster screen. Pews have replaced the chairs, and new stained glass windows were installed during the period from 1931 to 1935.

The current name of the church was taken in 1959 when the members of two historic Methodist churches of different ancestry, which had entered the United Church of Canada in 1925, were brought together as one congregation. While Sherbourne Street Methodist was of Wesleyan roots, Carlton Street United had a Primitive Methodist background.

Before the decision was made to amalgamate the

One wonders at the daring of the crew of builders from St. Hyacinthe who hoisted some tonnes of organ chests, reservoirs, expression boxes and pipes from the floor to the organ loft. The organ screen is constructed of steel reinforced plaster.

The 1886 west façade of Saint Luke's United Church is a masterful composition of towers, turrets, and articulated stonework. A new porch, added in 1960, has compromised the compositional integrity of the original.

two congregations, plans to make the church smaller were discussed. Mr. Edwin Northrup of Casavant Frères wrote to Toronto acoustician Prof. V. L. Henderson:

> This organ had extremely careful and detailed handling in design by Messrs. Kemp and [organist G.D.] Atkinson, collaborating with our Mr. Stoot. At that time, the church was enlarged, and the organ which is not a large organ was scaled to overcome the defect of a small organ for a large room. By "scaling" I refer to the diameter of the pipes, the progression throughout the compass, the voicing and the pressure. Everything was done for a large room.

Hence the high wind pressures of 5", 6" and 10" water manometer. The organ, 50 feet above the nave, is able to surround the congregation with organ tone.

In 1977 the organist was Jack Hillier. Plans for an extensive tonal revision initiated by Mr. Northrup in 1961 were prepared. In 1980, new mixtures were ordered and a reduced revision of pipework was begun, retaining the high wind pressures. Further revisions in the Choir organ were carried out during the tenure of Juergen Petrenko, organist from 1978 to 1983.

This organ has a curious feature, namely, the Corridor Diapason on the Great Organ, which is intended to bring the choir in, singing the processional hymn in time and on pitch.

1. *A History of Sherbourne Street,* Ernest Edmondson

Casavant Organ Opus 1356, 1929

GREAT ORGAN

		FEET	PIPES
	w.p. 5"		
1	Double Open Diapason	16	68
2	Violin Diapason	8	68
3	Hohlflote	8	68
4	Octave	4	68
5	Harmonic flute	4	68
6	Twelfth	2-2/3	61
7	Superoctave	2	61
8*	Mixture IV-V	1-1/3	293
	Tuba (from Choir)	8	—
	Chimes 25 notes		
	Harp (from Choir)		
9	Corridor Diapason	8	61

SWELL ORGAN (EXPRESSIVE) w.p. 5"

10	Lieblich Gedeckt	16	68
11	Open Diapason	8	68
12	Stopped Diapason	8	68
13†	Gemshorn	8	68
14	Voix céleste GG	8	61
15†	Octave	4	61
16	Flauto Traverso	4	61
17	Piccolo	2	61
18*	Mixture IV	1	244
19	Cornopean	8	68
20	Oboe	8	68
21	Vox Humana	8	68
	Chimes (from Choir)		
	Harp (from Choir)		
	Tremulant		

CHOIR ORGAN (EXPRESSIVE) w.p. 6"

22	Geigen Principal	8	61
23	Melodia	8	61
24	Viol d'Orchestre	8	61
25	Lieblich Flöte	4	61
26†	Nazard	2-2/3	61
27†	Principal	2	61
28†	Tierce	1-3/5	61
29	Clarinet	8	61
30	Tuba (wind press. 10")	8	61
	Chimes (preparation)		
	Harp, Harp Sub		
	Tremulant		

PEDAL ORGAN

31	Double Open Diapason (12 independent quints)	32	12
32	Open Wood	16	32
33	Open Metal (from #1)	16	—
34	Bourdon	16	32
35	Gedeckt (from #10)	16	—
36†	Octave	8	32
37	Stopped Diapason (20 from #34)	8	12
38†	Choral Bass (20 from #36)	4	12
39	Trombone	16	32
40	Trumpet (20 from #39)	8	12

COUPLERS

Great, Swell, Choir to Pedal 8
Great, Swell to Pedal 4
Chimes to Pedal
Swell, Choir to Great16, 8, 4
Great 4
Swell 16, 4
Great to Choir 8
Swell to Choir 16, 8, 4
Choir 16, 4

ADJUSTABLE COMBINATIONS (CAPTURE TYPE)

Great	1 2 3 4			Thumb
Swell	1 2 3 4	5	6	Thumb
Choir	1 2 3 4			Thumb
Pedal	1 2 3			Thumb
General	1 2 3 4	5	6	Toe
General Cancel				Thumb
Adjuster				Thumb

REVERSIBLE PISTONS

Swell, Great, Choir to Pedal 8
Swell, Choir to Great 8
Swell to Choir 8
Full Organ

ANALYSIS

	STOPS	RANKS	PIPES	REAL STOPS
Great	9	13	816	9
Swell	12	15	914	13
Choir	9	9	488	9
Pedal	10	4	176	4
Totals	40	41	2,394	35

ACTION

Electro pneumatic, Ventil stop action.

†pipes moved
*new pipes 1980-83

104

THE CHURCH OF SAINT MARY MAGDALENE

477 Manning Avenue
Rebuild of Breckels and Matthews Organ, circa 1906

The parish of St. Mary Magdalene was founded in 1888 by the Reverend Charles Darling, then assistant curate of St. Matthias' Church, Bellwoods Avenue, and later the first rector of the new parish. The parish is named after St. Mary Magdalene's, Paddington, a church in London, England where Fr. Darling had earlier served as an assistant.

A plan for the church was prepared by the prominent Toronto architect Frank Darling, an elder brother of Fr. Charles Darling, both sons of a rector of the Church of the Holy Trinity. Other projects by Frank Darling's firm, Darling & Pearson, include Convocation Hall, the former Bank of Montreal, now the Sportsman's Hall of Fame, at Front and Yonge Streets, and the rebuilding of the Canadian Parliament Buildings after the fire of 1916.

Resources were very limited, and the church could only be developed in stages. A rather ambitious design for the completed church submitted by Frank Darling to the Vestry in 1892 has never been realized. A choir loft, added in 1920, freed up space in the chancel for liturgical rites. The organ console followed the choir to the new gallery in 1931, and the sanctuary was remodelled in 1931 and again in 1963.

The arrival of Healey Willan at St. Mary Magdalene in 1921 as Organist and Choirmaster was a pivotal event in the development of the liturgy of this parish church. It also left a lasting mark on music in many other Anglican churches and those of other denominations. Plainsong or Gregorian chant has been, and continues to be, used extensively in Solemn Masses. Willan composed a large quantity of music, and much of it was specifically directed for use in the context of the mass at St. Mary Magdalene. Except for a brief interruption, Healey Willan remained in this post until his death in 1968.

As the music of Willan served the mass, so do the church's architecture and the organ, today known as The Healey Willan Memorial Organ. The lively acoustics of the room have also contributed to the type of music that Willan was creating.

Although Frank Darling had studied with the most famous of the local Gothicists, including Henry Langley (Jarvis Street Baptist and Metropolitan United Churches), he

was an architect of more eclectic tastes. For St. Mary Magdalene he appears to have been influenced by the Romanesque, as evidenced by the rounded tops of doors and windows and the great arch between the nave and the sanctuary. On the other hand, the ceiling is not vaulted, but trussed. The church is rectangular in plan with a seven-sided apse placed at the east end. An arcade separates the higher nave from lower side aisles. The north aisle is considerably wider than the south aisle. The room is distinguished, above all, by its simplicity and openness.

Some of the stained glass windows, as well as the great rood cross were designed in 1921 by William Rae, a member of the congregation. Rae was an architect who had designed the renovations at St. Anne's Church in the 1920's which incorporated work of the Group of Seven. The 1963 renovations of the St. Mary Magdalene sanctuary were undertaken by Rambush & Company of New York.

Throughout Dr. Willan's tenure as organist at St. Mary's, the main windchests built by Breckels and Matthews contained a very serious design fault. No pipe valve could be repaired without the removal of at least thirty pipes. One attempt to repair three dead notes included two that were on the Swell Mixture; this meant that over 120 pipes had to be taken off the chest while top boards were unscrewed and lifted out. After re-leathering and adjusting the three offending valves, the boards were screwed down and pipes replaced only to find that one of the three notes was still dead. Fortunately, the said

The table or portative organ stands at the side of the church. Built by Karl Wilhelm, it has four octaves of flute pipes at eight foot pitch.

(Opposite) The interior of the Church of St. Mary Magdalene is volumetrically spacious, bounded by hard masonry surfaces. These are the ingredients which have given such a successful acoustic for choral and organ repertoire, and have inspired Healy Willan and others to add to this repertoire.

windchests were all removed during the rebuilding and replaced with new Pitman chests with valves easily serviceable by removal of the bottom boards.

All of the stops in the organ of Dr. Willan's time remain except the Great Diapason No. 1 and the Great Doppel Flute 8'. The Tuba 16' lower notes were not used, but an S. R. Warren Trombone 16' was brought from St. Andrew's Presbyterian Church and re-voiced with new tongues and new tops of tin to reduce the rattle of the zinc resonators.

The Church of St. Mary Magdalene ranks with St. James' Cathedral as one of the buildings in Toronto in which a satisfying acoustic is maintained when the church is full of people. The cubic volume of St. Mary's is not as large as that of the Cathedral, but the sense of surround and support for congregational singing is so good that there is often the longing for just one more verse – a wish that the hymn could go on and on. Some of the joy of such singing has been captured on recent CD recordings: "Healey Willan Live, Vol. 1" (Jamon, 1998) and "Healey Willan at the Church of St. Mary Magdalene, Toronto" (EMI for the RCCO, 1997). Much of the recording was done during festival services when the church would have been quite full, yet the reverberation time remains high.

There is no mystical reason why such a moderate-sized building could have such a good musical acoustic. Sound bounces around the room about thirty times per second. If it does not get snuffed on a piece of carpet or trapped under a pew or in a joint in the roof boards, then it bounces again and again. St. Mary's is a plaster box with minimal roof clutter and only enough pews for the regular congregation. The aisles are wide and the floors well varnished. Acousticians go to great lengths to measure the sound absorption coefficients of the materials of which a room is built, and of the contents, but do not seem to have a place to list the sound traps and the clutter.

ORIGINS, ADDITIONS

1906 Breckels and Matthews built a pneumatic action organ of about 29 ranks in the chancel.

1931 L. E. Morel electrified the action and moved the console to the gallery as requested by Dr. Willan. Additions were later made of an English-built Tuba 16' -8' -4' and the Choir Flute was unified by Franklin Legge to play at 4' pitch.

1971 The Healey Willan Memorial Fund was set up and rebuilding of the organ begun under organist Giles Bryant using volunteer help and builder David Legge.

1973 – 1980 Rebuilding carried out in stages using Casavant chests, pipes and installation and tonal finishing by Alan T. Jackson working on a time basis to allow for the diminishing volunteer force.

Rebuild of Breckels and Matthews Organ, circa 1906

GREAT ORGAN

		FEET	PIPES
1	Double Open Diapason	16	61
2	Open Diapason #1	8	61
3	Open Diapason #2 (ext.#1)	8	12
4*	Stopped Diapason	8	61
5	Gamba	8	61
6	Octave	4	61
7*	Wald Flute	4	61
8	Twelfth	2-2/3	61
9	Fifteenth	2	61
10*	Mixture IV	1-1/3	224
11*	Cornet Mid C V	8	185
12*	Trumpet	8	61
13*	Clarion	4	61
	Great 4' Coupler		

SWELL ORGAN (ENCLOSED)

		FEET	PIPES
14	Lieblich Bourdon	16	61
15	Stopped Diapason	8	61
16	Salicional	8	61
17	Viola da Gamba	8	61
18	Vox Angelica Ten C	8	49
19	Principal	4	61
20	Suabe Flute	4	61
21	Nazard	2-2/3	61
22	Flageolet	2	61
23	Tierce	1-3/5	61
24*	Sharp Mixture IV	1	244
25*	Bassoon L/2	16	61
26†	Trumpet	8	61
27†	Oboe	8	61
28†	Shawn	4	61
	Tremulant		
	Swell 16' coupler		
	Swell 4' coupler		

CHOIR ORGAN (ENCLOSED)

		FEET	PIPES
29	Gedackt	8	61
30	Dulciana	8	61
31	Unda Maris Ten C	8	49
32	Chimney Flute	4	61
33*	Spire Principal	2	61
34*	Larigot	1-1/3	61
35*	Cymbel III	1/2	183
36	Cremona	8	61
37	Tuba	8	61

Tremulant
Choir 16' coupler
Choir 4' coupler

PEDAL ORGAN

		FEET	PIPES
38	Sub Bourdon (wired from #40&#41)	32	—
39	Open Metal (from #1)	16	—
40	Open Wood	16	32
41	Subbass	16	32
42	Lieblich Bourdon (from #14)	16	—
43	Octave	8	32
44	Flute	8	32
45	Super Octave	4	32
46	Recorder	4	32
47*	Mixture IV	2-2/3	128
48†	Ophecleide	16	32
49	Bassoon (from #25)	16	—
50	Trumpet (from #12)	8	—
51	Clarion (from #13)	4	—

COUPLERS (TILTING TABLETS)

Great, Swell & Choir to Pedal 8 & 4
Swell, Choir to Great 16, 8 & 4
Swell to Choir 16, 8 & 4

ADJUSTABLE COMBINATION PISTONS (electronic, Grecar system)

Great, Swell, Choir, Pedal	6 Thumb
Generals	10 Thumb & Toe
General Cancel	Thumb
Adjuster	Thumb
Great & Pedal Combination Control	

REVERSIBLE PISTONS

Great to Pedal	Thumb & Toe
Swell, Choir to Pedal	Thumb
Swell, Choir to Great	Thumb
Swell to Choir	Thumb
Full Organ	Toe

*new pipes
†revoiced reeds

SAINT MICHAEL'S CATHEDRAL

200 Church Street
S. R. Warren & Son, 1880
Agreement of June 1880, Specification No. 3356

The picturesque dormers and spire which distinguish St. Michael's Cathedral are additions by architects Langely & Burke to a more somber original building designed by William Thomas.

(Overleaf) The S. R. Warren & Son Organ of 1880 in St. Michael's Cathedral. The graceful curved bands and the line of the pipe mouths reflect in contrary motion the curved roof trusses above.

While not the oldest Roman Catholic congregation in this city, St. Michael's is today the oldest house of worship of the denomination. Since its consecration on September 29, 1848, St. Michael's has been the official seat of the archbishop or, as at the present time, the cardinal archbishop.

When Bishop Michael Power became Bishop of Toronto in 1842, he was first based at St. Paul's R. C. Church (now Basilica) on Power Street. The year before, the Roman Catholic See of Kingston had been divided into two, with the western portion becoming the Diocese of Toronto. In 1845 he bought a "park lot," located at the northern edge of York at the edge of the forest. To the south was McGill Square which some twenty-five years later became the site of Metropolitan United Church, much to the chagrin of members of St. Michael's.

In 1841 the English Gothicist, A.W. N. Pugin, published his book *The True Principles of Pointed or Christian Architecture*. This treatise established the Gothic Style as the only acceptable architecture for Christian churches.

That same year William Thomas arrived in York from England, and noted in his writings that "the places of worship are very neatly built with some pretense to Classic architecture in brick and stone, scarcely any Gothic use in this country. Houses of wood with the Roman orders."[1]

Thomas quickly gained respect as an architect and gained a number of significant commissions including St. Michael's Cathedral, St. Paul's Anglican Cathedral in London, and Christ's Church, Hamilton. His masterpiece is generally considered to be St. Andrew's Presbyterian Church on James Street, Hamilton, today known as St. Paul's Church.

For Bishop Michael Power, William Thomas developed a large plan under a single pitched roof. The interior was dark and sober, and, like all of his churches, was highlighted by a rich neo-mediæval decoration. Some thirty years later, the firm of Langley & Burke was called in by Bishop Lynch to complete the cathedral bell tower and renovate the interior. The dormer windows were introduced to admit more daylight. These new features add a quality of the picturesque to the composition

which detract from the more mature Gothic of the bell tower and spire.

Inside, the main room is essentially a hall church; it consists of one volumetric space of approximately the same height. The triforium arches which Thomas had included along the two column lines have been developed to simulate clerestory windows. But only minimal natural light passes from the dormer windows above the side aisles into the nave. A redecoration of the interior in 1937 by Messrs. Weekes and Warne placed "up-light" luminaries below these arches in a manner reminiscent of flower boxes, and tracery within the openings. A viewer has only to recollect the exterior massing of the church to realize that these are *not* clerestory windows.

There are some exceptional assemblies of stained glass. The great east window which provides the visual backdrop to the high altar was imported by Bishop de Charbonnel in 1858. The artist who prepared the image of Christ on the Cross surrounded by Mary his mother, Mary Magdalene, his disciple John, Joseph of Arimathea and Nicodemus was Etienne Thevenot who also provided some of the stained glass for Notre Dame de Paris.

On July 26, 1880 an agreement was signed by S. R. Warren & Son and John Joseph Lynch, Archbishop of Toronto for the Roman Catholic Episcopal Corporation of the Diocese of Toronto, to construct and install a gallery organ in the Cathedral. "The case to be made of chestnut ornamented with Black Walnut mouldings. The front pipes to be ornamented in Gold and Colors. The design to be in accordance with that as submitted and approved... [and] to erect the same in St. Michael's Cathedral in the said City of Toronto – and also to attach thereto a water-motor of sufficient capacity to furnish an adequate supply of wind to said organ, with a water pressure of fifty pounds to the square inch, and also an Auxiliary Bellows for the same, the whole to be supplied and placed in position on or before the seventh day of September 1880." Later in the document "the said parties of the second part further agree and bind themselves to conduct the water motor aforesaid and to provide proper sewage for the exhaust water at their own cost and expense." The cost of the organ was $7,500.00 paid over five years.

The organ is probably the most important surviving example of S. R. Warren's work in Ontario. However, in September of 1993 the organ was closed, covered and bridged-over with scaffolding to protect it from construction work. It was later found that the gallery floor was structurally unsafe. The gallery and organ have been out of bounds ever since. The organ which had played weekly, almost without exception, for over 110 years was silent.

Except for the pump handle that used to project from the side of the organ case, the whole wind system remains as it was, the main reservoir and feeders beneath, the "Auxiliary Bellows" in the tower with its two feeders and rocking bar still connected to the vertical shaft of the double-acting water motor. A slow speed centrifugal organ blower has been blowing the organ for most of the century.

In 1962 the organ was tonally revised by Kney and Bright of London, Ontario and supplied with five new reservoirs to bypass the original, single main reservoir. A new electric slider chest was added in space behind the main organ to provide five new pedal stops.

The instrument does not appear to have suffered from being closed down and would respond well to restoration to the way it was before 1962 with the old wind system made operative. The new pipes could be retained or replaced with copies of the originals. The key action of the Swell Organ was always heavy and slack because of a long horizontal run of trackers. The Swell Organ is behind the Great and Choir and is at a higher level. The original combination action is still in place but the toe levers have been borrowed to operate couplers and to free stop knobs for use with the added Pedal electric slider chest.

Students of St. Michael's Choir School before 1993 gained valuable experience practising on the three imperfect instruments at hand. A small Walcker two-manual-and-pedal tracker organ in the Cathedral Chapel has very limited resources and an insensitive action. The auditorium organ has a comfortable 1959 three-manual Casavant console and Choir Organ playing a 1916 Casavant theatre organ with some added stops. The test for students was to practise and to play for services on the 1880 tracker organ in the Cathedral, an experience no less difficult than playing the ancient organs of Europe.

1. *Hallowed Walls: Church Architecture of Upper Canada*, Marion MacRae, Anthony Adamson

S. R. Warren & Son, 1880
Agreement of June 1880,
Specification No. 3356

GREAT ORGAN

		FEET	PIPES
1 Double Open Diapason			
	METAL	16	58
2 Open Diapason	METAL	8	58
3 Dolce	METAL	8	58
4 Doppel Flute	WOOD	8	58
5 Gamba	METAL	8	58
6 Principal	METAL	4	58
7 Violina or Boehm flute (built as Boehm fl)			
	METAL	4	58
8 Twelfth	METAL	2-2/3	58
9 Fifteenth	METAL	2	58
10 Sesquialtera III	METAL		174
11 Mixture V	METAL		290
12 Trumpet	METAL	8	58
13 Clarion	METAL	4	58

SWELL ORGAN (ENCLOSED)

14 Bourdon	WOOD	16	58
15 Open Diapason	METAL	8	58
16 Stopped Diapason	WOOD	8	58
17 Viol D Gamba	METAL	8	58
18 Traverse Flute	WOOD	4	58
19 Octave	METAL	4	58
20 Fugara	METAL	4	58
21 Fifteenth	METAL	2	58
22 Mixture III	METAL		174
23 Horn	METAL	8	58
24 Cor Anglais (built as Clarinet Ten C 16, 46 pipes)	METAL	8	58
25 Oboe	METAL	8	58
26 Vox Humana (in separate Swell)	METAL	8	58
27 Clarion	METAL	4	58

CHOIR ORGAN

28 Geigen Principal	METAL	8	58
29 Dulciana	METAL	8	58
30 Gedackt Flute	WOOD	8	58
31 Flute D'Amour	WOOD	4	58
32 Harmonic Flute	METAL	4	58
33 Violina	METAL	4	58
34 Piccolo	METAL	2	58
35 Clarinet	METAL	8	58
36 Hautbois French	METAL	8	58

PEDAL ORGAN

37 Double Open	WOOD	16	30
38 Double Dulciana	WOOD	16	30
39 Violincello	METAL	8	30
40 Contra Posaunne	METAL	16	30

MECHANICAL REGISTERS

41 Coupler Swell to Great
42 Coupler Swell to Choir
43 Coupler Swell to Pedal
44 Coupler Great to Pedal
45 Coupler Choir to Pedal
46 Bellows Signal
    Tremolo to Swell

COMBINATION PEDALS
TO GREAT ORGAN

1 Draws Nos. 3 & 7 Returning all others
2 Draws Nos. 2, 3, 4, 5, 6, 7, Returning all others
3 Full Great Organ
    Three Combination Pedals to Swell Organ

Kney and Bright, Pipe Organ Builders, 1962
Tonal changes and additions

GREAT ORGAN
Doppel flute 8 of wood replaced by a Rohrflote 8 of metal.
Gamba 8 replaced by a Terz 1-3/5
Mixture V replaced by a Mixture IV 2'
Sesquialtera III replaced by a Cymbel III 1/2"

SWELL ORGAN
Mixture III replaced by a Nazard 2-2/3'
Vox Humana 8 replaced by a Mixture III

CHOIR ORGAN
Flute D'Amour 4 replaced by a Principal 4
Violina 4 replaced by a Quinte 1-1/3'
Clarinet 8 replaced by a Sesquialtera II from Ten C
Cor Anglais 8 (old Swell) replaced by a Krummhorn 8 Ten C

PEDAL ORGAN
Gedackt 8 on new chest, 30 pipes
Flute 4 on new chest, 30 pipes
Rohrflote 2 on new chest, 30 pipes
Mixture IV 5 1/3' on new chest, 120 pipes
Schalmey 4' on new chest, 30 pipes
Combination toe pedals disconnected and used to register couplers.

SAINT PAUL'S ANGLICAN CHURCH

227 Bloor Street East
Casavant Organ Opus 550, built 1914, new console and revisions 1955

Fine sculptural and architectural details are a hallmark of St. Paul's Bloor Street, one of the largest Churches in Canada.

St. Paul's Anglican Church, Bloor Street, was constructed between 1909 and 1913 to a design by Edward James Lennox. This architect had already had a distinguished career and had designed Toronto Old City Hall (c. 1899), the King Edward Hotel (c. 1902), and in 1905 the Bank of Toronto at 205 Yonge Street (today the home of the Toronto Historical Board). In 1903 Lennox had been retained by the Vestry of St. Paul's to alter and expand their 1858-60 building in order to provide for the needs of the church's growing congregation. (The latter portion of the complex, today known as Cody Hall, was built in 1928.)

The historical record indicates that E. J. Lennox, upon being invited to prepare a design for the new $150,000 house of worship, agreed but "insisted that his work be accepted as a contribution to the building fund."[1] While Lennox had designed buildings in a wide range of styles, for this assignment he chose a High Victorian Gothic vocabulary which marries well with the earlier building. Both buildings seem to respond to the influence of the English Gothicist, A. W. N. Pugin.

The original drawings show an imposing tower at the north-east corner of the building which provides a vertical counterpoint to the horizontal mass of the earlier church to the west. While this additional element was likely deleted from the final design for cost reasons, had it been built it might have afforded a presence which today is lacking in spite of the size of the nave. The nave is 14 metres (46 feet) wide and 46 metres (152 feet) long. It rises to a height of 28 metres (92 feet). The wide transepts allow two-thirds of the congregation (capacity intended to be 2500) to be seated within 21 metres (70 feet) of the pulpit.[2] These transepts and the chancel area are equal in height to the nave and this sheer volume of captured space contributes to a remarkable resonance, without equal in this city.

The organ was donated by Mrs. T. Gibbs Blackstock and Family in memory of Thomas Gibbs Blackstock, K.C. When Dr. Healey Willan played for the dedication in April 1914, it was believed to be the fifth largest organ in the world. St. Paul's, London and Westminster Abbey had only 77 stops, while St. Paul's, Toronto had 106.

The consultant for the first design, c.1906, was T. J. Palmer, who asked to have the

responsibility passed on to the English consultant Lt. Col. George Dixon who had worked with Palmer at St. Nicholas Church, Whitehaven, Cumbria. The English influence for this organ was considerable and Dixon listed 18 ranks of reeds that were to be "voiced in England under the direction of Lt. Col. Dixon and his choice of voicer to be accepted by the builders, provided cost does not exceed $2730. for the whole."[3]

It has often been said that it is the consultants, and not the organ builders, who set the trends in organ building. Clause 21 of the original contract of December 22, 1910 states that "The String section on the Orchestral is to produce the same effects as the string section in the Hope-Jones Organ in St. Paul's Church, Buffalo." Hope-Jones was the designer of the Wurlitzer Theatre organ officially called the "Hope-Jones Unit Orchestra." The next clause in the St. Paul contract, No. 22 reads, "The organ, when finished, to be inspected and passed upon, by Lt. Col. George Dixon, of

(Opposite) There are thirty three ranks of pipes in the gallery organ, all contained in one very large expression box. None of the pipes in this façade speak. If they did, they would be notes in the sixteen foot range, normal diapason tone from the towers and extremely keen string tone from the centre pipes.

(Above) View of St. Paul's Bloor Street from the gardens of the Manulife Insurance Company across the street through a sculpture by Kirk Newman.

England; the organist of the church, or any competent authority appointed by the Chairman of the Organ Committee."

The origin of the various ranks of reeds was clarified when Edwin D. Northrup wrote in preparation for the International Congress of Organists in 1967:

The original seating capacity of St. Paul's Church was 2500 which was reported to be the same as that of Sir Christopher Wren's St. Paul's Cathedral in London. In the course of the 1991 renovations which moved the font to its current location, seating was reduced to 1800.

Healey Willan has told all who will listen that Arthur Harrison made ALL the reeds and actually Harrison and Harrison "made the Trompette Harmonique and Clarion 4 in Tuba Organ." They gave a price of something like 27 pounds, and later sent Dixon a bill for experiments. I recall the letter said 'Harry (brother of Arthur) and I have finally got our costs together on the experimental trumpet for St. Paul's.' Dixon

The east loft (above) contains the Great and Swell Organs, both double-decked and also the Pedal Open Diapason 32' and Bourdon 16' pipes.

The west loft (right, inset) contains the Choir, Orchestral and Tuba Organs and also the Pedal 32' Reeds and Contrabass 16' and percussions.

The stops in the left side jamb (right) visible here, are those of the Swell, Pedal and Echo Organs. The manual key covering is ivory.

refused to pay and was furious and his handwriting showed it. But J. C. Casavant paid it and they incurred a loss of $1300 alone on the reeds. The Great Reeds were to be mitred and hooded and toned like St. Paul's, Edinburgh. Northrup also explains "The Bombardon 32', Ophecleide 16' and Posaune 8' were from Jones and Blossom, and were made by the late William Gyples Jones, who only this year died at the age of 92. He was a choir boy under Robert Hope Jones at Birkenhead, and through Hope Jones (no relation) got into the organ business, and has taught most of the fine reed voicers in England, with the exception of Willis. This was the FIRST metal 32' made in England and was to be 'like Carlisle Cathedral carried down an octave'. Cost 88 pounds! Jones also did the Great Reeds 16-8-4, the Swell Trumpets 16-8-4, the Tuba Sonora and Quint Trombone 5 1/3'. Mr. Frank Wesson was a Willis voicer who did a bit of moonlighting to put bread on his table, and so the old man sacked him. At the time, Dixon wrote that he did not think Wesson's slight hearing defect would hinder him and he voiced the Tuba Trombone 16, the Tuba Mirabilis and Clarion.

In 1956 a new four-manual console given in memory of Mrs. T. G. Blackstock by her family was installed and a tonal revision and mechanical restoration was supervised by E. D. Northrup of Casavant and organist Dr. Charles Peaker. None of the English reeds were changed nor were they changed during the subsequent revisions of 1981-82 when the organ was cleaned and partially revoiced under the direction of organist John Tuttle and Alan T. Jackson. New expression shutters were added to direct sound of the Swell Organ to the chancel and the canvas dust cover over the Great Organ was changed to

fiberglass to reflect sound. The remote, electro-pneumatic note relays and combination machines were replaced with a Corlis solid-state system to improve the response of the action. Soon after, in 1985 a recording[4] dedicated to Ross B. Elliot was made by John Tuttle featuring the *Introduction, Passacaglia and Fugue*, composed in 1916 by Dr. Willan for the St. Paul's organ.

During 1991 the organ was shut down for a major revision of the chest action and wind system. All of the manual windchests were converted from Ventil stop action to Pitman action. This increased the responsiveness of the key action and allowed the fitting of schwimmer wind controls. The larger wind reservoirs were then disconnected or removed and the noise from the high pressure organ wind became almost inaudible.

Only the Echo Organ in the gallery retains the original action and wind system. Even the hand-wound electric chest magnets remain in use. The original four-manual console has been moved to the gallery and will be made operative by 2002 when new electronic controls will be installed for the whole organ. Organist Eric Robertson will use it as an Antiphonal accompaniment when the choir sings from the gallery. For 45 years the console stood in the basement choir room where Dr. Peaker used to do silent practice. "I still practise on it – 'heard melodies are sweet, but those unheard are sweeter'. As its cadences roll through my mind I think of the men who have played it; Hollins and Vierne, those blind virtuosi from Edinburgh and Paris; Farnam, Dupré, MacMillan, Sir William McKie of the Abbey and my own distinguished predecessors – Maitland Farmer, the Late T. J. Crawford, and that most eminent musician, Dr. Healey Willan. Nor could I forget Dr. Alexander Davies who filled in so well at each interregnum."[5]

CHANGES AND ADDITIONS

1914 Organ installed, 4 manuals, 106 stops, 116 ranks.

1955 New console and remote coupler & combination actions and tonal revisions, 23 ranks of new pipes, new chest magnets except for Echo Organ.

1970-76 Organ leathering replaced as needed.

1981 Organ cleaned, new Corlis solid state couplers and combination action installed, new chancel-side Swell shutters added, minor revoicing of flues, reeds restored, blowers overhauled.

1991 All main wind chests except the Echo converted to Pitman type action and schwimmer winding, new Great Cymbale chest, Swell and Pedal reeds cleaned and all flues and reeds regulated.

1996 Re-leathered all console combination pneumatics.

1. "Lennox gave plans for St. Paul's Church," *Mail and Empire*, 19th April, 1933.
2. *Edward James Lennox Builder of Toronto*, Marilyn M. Litvak.
3. Contract, Casavant F.L. 1910.
4. Frank Cairns of St. Paul's produced the LP record, WRCI-4968. A CD version was made in 1989 by Gothic Records Inc. G 48629.
5. Dr. Charles Peaker, *The Globe & Mail*, Nov 24, 1956.

Casavant Organ Opus 550, built 1914, new console and revisions 1955

	GREAT ORGAN	FEET	PIPES
1	Gross Geigen	16	61
2	Diapason I (old No. 2)	8	61
3	Diapason II (old No. 3)	8	61
4	Geigen Principal	8	61
5	Waldflote	8	61
6	Rohrflote	8	61
7	Spitzflote	8	61
8	Quintflote	5-1/3	61
9	Octave	4	61
10	Geigen Octave	4	61
11	Flute Triangulaire	4	61
12*	Flute Ouverte	4	61
13	Octave Quinte	2-2/3	61
14	Super Octave	2	61
15*	Fourniture IV	1-1/3	244
16*	Cymbale III	1/2	183
17	Contra Tromba	16	61
18	Tromba	8	61
19	Octave Tromba	4	61
	Tuba to Great		
	Great Super		
	Great Unison Off		
	Chimes from Orchestral		
	Harp from Orchestral		
	Célesta from Choir		

	SWELL ORGAN (ENCLOSED)		
20	Double Stopped Diapason	16	73
21	Horn Diapason	8	73
22	Stopped Diapason	8	73
23	Viola da Gamba	8	73
24	Voix Céleste (1-12 new 1955)	8	73
25	Octave Gamba	4	73
26	Lieblichflote	4	73
27	Flautina	2	61
28*	Plein Jeu V	2	305
29	Oboe	8	73
30	Vox Humana	8	73
	Tremulant		
31	Double Trumpet	16	73
32	Trumpet	8	73
33	Clarion	4	73
	Tuba Organ Coupler		
	Swell Sub		
	Swell Unison Off		
	Swell Super		
	Chimes from Orchestral		
	Harp from Orchestral		
	Celesta from Choir		

	CHOIR ORGAN (ENCLOSED)		
34*	Quintaton	16	73
35	Spitzprincipal	8	73
36	Cor de Nuit (new 1962)	8	73
37	Viole de Gambe	8	73
38	Salicional	8	73
39	Vox Angelica Ten. C	8	61
40	Spitzflote	4	73
41	Zauberflote	4	73
42*	Nazard (new chest)	2-2/3	61
43*	Blockflote (new chest)	2	61
44	Tierce	1-3/5	61
45*	Larigot (new chest)	1-1/3	61
46*	Sifflote (new chest)	1	61
47*	Zimbel IV	1	244
48	Contra Fagotto	16	73
49	Clarinet	8	73
	Tremulant		
	Tuba Organ Coupler		
	Choir Sub		
	Choir Unison Off		
	Choir Super		
	Harp from Orchestral		

50 Celesta
    Chimes from Orchestral

ORCHESTRAL ORGAN (ENCLOSED)
51 Contre Viole   16   73
52 Flute Harmonique   8   73
53 Quintaton   8   73
54 Viole d'Orchestre   8   73
55 Viole Céleste Ten. C 8   61
56 Concert Flute
    Harmonique   4   73
57 Viole Octaviante   4   73
58 Piccolo Harmonique   2   61
59 Cornet
    de Violes III   2-2/3   183
60 Corno de Bassetto   16   73
61 Cor Anglais   8   73
62 Hautbois d'Orchestre 8   73
    Tremulant
    Tuba Organ Coupler
    Orchestral Sub
    Orchestral Unison Off
    Orchestral Super
63 Chimes   25
64 Harp   44
    Celesta from Choir

TUBA ORGAN
(ENCLOSED WITH ORCHESTRAL)
65 Principal   4   61
66 Grand Fourniture
    V   2   305
67 Trombone   16   61
68 Tuba Sonora   8   61
69 Trompette
    Harmonique   8   61
70 Quinte Horn   5-1/3   61
71 Clarion Harmonique   4   61
72 Tuba Mirabilis
    (unenclosed)   8   61
73 Tuba Clarion
    (unenclosed)   4   61

ECHO GREAT (ENCLOSED)
74 Contra Gamba   16   73
75 Open Diapason   8   73
76 Salicional   8   73
77 Harmonic Flute   4   73
78 Horn   8   73

ECHO SWELL
(ENCLOSED WITH ECHO GREAT)
79 Viole de Gambe   8   73

80 Voix Céleste Ten. C 8   61
81 Gedackt   8   73
82* Erzahler   8   73
83 Unda Maris Ten. C   8   61
84 Lieblichflote   4   73
85 Dolce Cornet V   8   341
86 Contra Oboe   16   73
    Tremulant

ECHO PEDAL (ENCLOSED)
87 Diapason   16   32
88 Gamba (from #74)   16   —
89 Bourdon   16   32

PEDAL ORGAN
90 Double Open
    Diapason   32   28
    (4 polyphonic)
91 Diapason (from #90) 16   12
92 Subbass   16   32
93* Contrebass   16   32
94 Geigen (from #1)   16   —
95 Viole (from #51)   16   —
96 Gedackt (from #20) 16   —
97 Quintaton
    (from #34)   16   —
98* Gemshornquint   10-2/3   32
99 Octave   8   32
100* Principal (ext. #93) 8   12
101 Viole Octave
    (from #51)   8   —
102 Stopped Flute
    (ext #92)   8   12
103 Still Gedackt
    (from #20)   8   —
104* Octave Quinte
    (ext #98)   5-1/3   12
105 *Superoctave
    (ext #99)   4   12
106* Choralbass (ext #93) 4   12
107* Flute (ext #92)   4   12
108* Blockflote
    (new chest)   2   32
109 Fourniture III
    (new chest)   2   96
110* Harmonics II   1-3/5   64
111 Bombardon   32   32
112 Ophecleide
    (ext #111)   16   12
113 Trombone
    (from #67)   16   —
114 Posaune (ext #111)   8   12
115 Clarion (ext #111)   4   12

    Tuba Organ Coupler
    Harp from Orchestral
    Chimes from Orchestral
    Celesta from Choir

COUPLERS (IN TABLETS)
Great, Swell, Choir, Orch. to Pedal
    Unison, Super
Tuba to Pedal Unison
Swell, Choir, Orch to Great Sub,
    Unison, Super
Swell, Orch. to Choir Sub,
    Unison, Super
Choir, Orch. to Swell Unison
Swell, Choir to Orch. Unison
Echo Couplers (in stop knobs)
Echo Great and Swell to Pedal
Unison, Super
Echo Swell to Echo Great Sub,
Unison, Super
Echo to 4th Manual Unison
Echo Great Sub, Super
Echo Swell Sub, Unison off, Super
Echo Couplers to Main Organ
Echo Pedal to Pedal
Echo Great to Great
Echo Great to Choir
Echo Swell to Great
Echo Swell to Swell
Echo On, Main Organ Off
reversible tablet and piston
Echo On tablet

ORDER OF KEYBOARDS
Orchestral (upper)
Swell
Great
Choir (lower)
Balanced Pedals (in order, right to
left)
Crescendo, Orch. & Tuba, Swell,
Choir, Echo
Indicators
Full Organ
Crescendo
Wind, Voltmeter
Swell Nave Shutters On Light
Adjustable Combination Pistons
Corlis Solid State System, 16 levels
Generals - 12 thumb, 1-10
duplicated on toe
Pedal - 6 thumb and toe pistons
Great, Swell, Choir, Orch - 6

thumb pistons
Tuba 4 thumb pistons
Echo Great, Swell 2 thumb
pistons
General cancel piston
Adjuster
Reversible Pistons
Great to Pedal thumb and toe
Swell, Choir, Orch, Tuba to Pedal
thumb
Swell, Choir, Orch., Tuba to Great
thumb
Orch. to Swell thumb
Swell to Choir thumb
Full Organ thumb and toe
Great and Pedal Combination
rocker button

ANALYSIS

	STOPS	RANKS	PIPES	REAL STOPS
Great	19	24	1464	19
Swell	14	18	1242	14
Choir	16	19	1279	16
Orchestral	12	14	974	12
Tuba	9	13	793	9
Pedal	26	12	500	9
Echo Great	5	5	365	5
Echo Swell	8	12	780	8
Echo Pedal	3	2	64	2
Totals	112	119	7461	94

*New pipes in 1955

119

SAINT PAUL'S BASILICA

83 Power Street
R. S. Williams & Sons Co. Limited, Toronto circa 1898

The 1898 R. S. Williams Organ in St. Paul's Basilica. The organ is original in every respect.

St. Paul's is the oldest Roman Catholic congregation in Toronto, formerly named York. It was founded in 1822, when the town of York had 189 wooden houses and a population of 1,336. For the next twenty-four years it remained the only Roman Catholic house of worship in Toronto. For six years leading up to the consecration of St. Michael's Cathedral, St. Paul's was the *de facto* cathedral for Toronto's first bishop, the Most Reverend Michael Power, in the new Diocese of Western Ontario.

The present building was erected between 1887 and 1889. The architect was Joseph Connolly who, soon after his arrival from Limerick, had produced a masterful 14th century French Gothic design for the Cathedral Church of our Lady of the Immaculate Conception in Guelph (1863-1926). Between 1870 and 1890 Connolly had produced designs for a number of other Roman Catholic churches. Also noteworthy are St. Peter's Basilica, London and St. Mary's, Bathurst Street, Toronto.

For St. Paul's, Joseph Connolly developed a basilican plan based on 15th century Italian Renaissance precedents. This move away from the prevalent Gothic style used for religious architecture of the time was both daring and brilliant. A barrel-vaulted central nave ends at the east end in a wide apse for the high altar. Over the sanctuary an unknown Belgian artist has depicted the "Conversion of St. Paul" – one of many paintings adorning the interior. Shallow transepts face smaller apses on either side of the high altar. The organ and choir are placed in a gallery at the opposing end. Arcades in the Ionic Order separate this nave from north and south side aisles not quite two-thirds the height of the main body of the church.

Ample natural light illuminates the room, primarily from rows of arched clerestory windows set in the wall above the arcades. The tripartite façade clearly delineates the volumetrics of the room within, using classical orders and Roman arches. St. Paul's "has been likened to the 15th-century Santa Maria Novella in Florence, with the green and white marble of that edifice re-created here in rough Credit Valley stone and smooth Cleveland limestone. The light-filled interior displays all the lucidity and sense of visual order inimitably associated with the Renaissance."

The distinguished architect and historian, Eric Arthur, has regardeded the interior of St. Paul's as the most beautiful church interior in Toronto.[1] Many would agree.

The 39 metre (129 feet) "campanile" included in Connolly's design for the building was not completed

The console at St. Paul's Basilica. Note the flat pedalboard and the varied length of the sharps. The white indicator to the right of the name plate shows the level of the reservoir.

until 1907. The church is cherished by its parishioners and over recent years great sums have been expended to maintain its condition and enhance its beauty and usefulness as a place of worship. In 1898 the R. S. Williams & Sons organ was installed. The organ may have been built previously for another church and moved to St. Paul's in 1898. Williams' retail business was in Toronto from 1879 when it was renamed R. S. Williams & Son.[2] The name on the console adds "s" which was a late form, so the organ was built after 1879 and before 1898. No documents have been found relating to the purchase of the organ. The Williams factory was in Oshawa where they built many thousands of pianos, possibly 67,000, before they succumbed to the Depression in 1929. All of the other Toronto Williams organs have been rebuilt or removed. An original R. S. Williams is in use in Trinity Anglican Church, Colborne.

Most of the cases had wooden panels carved in low relief. Another earmark of the organs was the use of yellow ochre and clear varnish to finish the wooden pipes. The reeds were usually imported from France.

Whoever voiced the flue pipes had an unfortunate way of nicking the flues. Instead of pressing the "teeth" into the languid, the teeth went into the lower lip as well, causing the wind sheet to spread out. The pipes all sound a bit woolly and unfocused. Nevertheless, the Williams pipe organs were finely built.

In 1977 the organ was restored by Gabriel Kney & Co. of London, Ontario. Names of some of the builders and the date 1898 were found at that time on the inside panel of one of the wind chests. The Great Trumpet and Swell Oboe were imported from France and have the typical French blocks of Cavaillé-Coll reeds. The resonators of the trumpet are made of tin.

1 *Toronto No Mean City*, Eric Arthur, p 187
2 *Encyclopedia of Music in Canada*, p. 1002.

R. S. Williams & Sons Co. Limited, Toronto, circa 1898

GREAT ORGAN (58 NOTES)

Open Diapason (17 en façade)	8
Dulciana	8
Salicional (12 en façade)	8
Melodia	8
Principal	4
Flute d'Amour	4
Twelfth	2-2/3
Fifteenth	2
Mixture I – IV	1-1/3
Trumpet	8

SWELL ORGAN (58 NOTES ENCLOSED)

Bourdon Ten C	16
Open Diapason	8
Stopped Diapason	8
Concert Flute (12 common with Open Diapason)	8
Aeoline	8
Vox Celeste Ten C	8
Harmonic Flute	4
Violina	4
Harmonic Piccolo	2
Oboe – Bassoon	8

Vox Humana	8
Tremulant	

PEDAL ORGAN (30 NOTES)

Open Diapason	16
Bourdon	16

COUPLERS
Great To Pedal
Swell to Pedal
Swell to Great

COMPOSITION PEDALS
3 toe levers to Great, right side
2 toe levers to Swell, left side
Great to Pedal reversible

The composition of the Great Mixture is:

CC	F18	f30	f42
1-1/3	2	2-2/3	4
	1-1/3	2	2-2/3
		1-1/3	2
			1-1/3

122

SAINT SOSA LEE

296 Judson Street
Halbert Gober, 1995

It has become increasingly difficult to build churches in the City of Toronto because of the proliferation of building codes and zoning regulations. Also, residential neighbourhoods are becoming increasingly hostile to having new churches developed in their midst.

A local Korean Roman Catholic congregation addressed these problems in a novel way. Under the supervision of founding pastor Father Bernard Lee, the congregation purchased a modern indus-

St. Sosa Lee R. C. Church. Halbert Gober Organ. Any one organ pipe on speech sets its neighbour resonating. By arranging the pipes on the windchests and façade in major thirds, the builder has assisted the attack and blend of the pipes when playing major triads.

trial building located not too far off the Gardiner Expressway near Islington Avenue. The site has good access, a voluminous existing building, ample parking – the ingredients that every church could hope for. The building is virtually indistinguishable from its neighbours and more visibility might have been beneficial. Toronto architect Stephen Teeple skillfully reshaped this Ontario Hydro warehouse into a new church consecrated to the 19th century Korean Martyr, St. Sosa Lee. The project includes a spacious parish hall, offices and a rectory.

The main worship space is a large square into which natural light enters through a large skylight placed over the altar. The industrial origins are clearly spelled out in the exposed roof structure overhead, but one is astonished by the transformation that has taken place in the building.

A clear window behind this altar provides views of a dramatic arrangement of boulders on a grassy hillock, all within a protected courtyard. The sanctuary also contains a large wood and steel crucifix bearing a white plaster Corpus Christi by the artist Raphael Chang. The perimeter of the room is defined by a set of stations of the cross, carved in wood by Father Herman Falke.

Seating is provided on movable chairs. Additional height has been achieved by dropping the level of the floor slab below grade level. This not only provides an overview of the space from the entrance, but also has been used by the architect to provide a side gallery behind glass from which the proceedings can be shared by mothers with vocal babies and restless children. The church hall abuts this gallery area.

The organ sits at the back of the room at a slight angle to the rear wall. While the concrete floor has been covered with thin carpet, the acoustics are good, though not overly reverberant. The preponderance of 8' stops is appropriate in the somewhat dry acoustic and, at the same time, is well suited to the performance of 19th and 20th century music.

Halbert Gober, 1995

MANUAL I
Praestant	8'
Viola da Gamba (Man II)	8'
Octave	4'
Principal	2'
Mixture	III

MANUAL II
Bourdon	8'
Viola da Gamba	8'
Celeste	8'
Flauto Traverso	4'
Octavin	2'
Cornet	II
Trumpet	8'

PEDAL
Subbass	16'
Subbass	8'
(from Bourdon 8')	
Trombone	16'
Trumpet	8'
(from Trumpet 8')	

COUPLERS
II/I, I/P & II/P
Pedal Super Coupler
Pedal Unison Off

Mechanical key and stop action. All stops except Praestant 8' (façade) are under expression. 94mm (3-3/4") wind pressure. Façade pipe layout is in traditional major thirds.

SAINT THOMAS'S
ANGLICAN CHURCH

383 Huron Street
Guilbault-Thérien, Inc., Opus 37, 1991, rebuild of Casavant 1911,
S. R. Warren 1885

St. Thomas's Anglican Church, Guilbault-Thérien Organ. The pipes displayed in the façade are of 75% polished tin.

The St. Thomas's Church building that we know today was built at lightning speed as a "temporary" building for a growing parish. The idea of relocating from a first building located at the intersection of Sussex and Huron Streets was first raised in June 1892. The building was designed in August, construction began on September 14, and the building was ready for use on January 17, 1893.

Eden Smith was not at the time a qualified member of the recently formed Ontario Association of Architects (1889), but as member of the parish he made an offer at the June 1892 Special Vestry to design a simple brick structure. This would tide the congregation over until a church of adequate dignity and permanence could be built.

The church in its first unadorned state was described as "a little bare looking at first," but was seen to offer a space cast in the tradition of the prevailing Gothic Revival of the times. In the design of St. Thomas's, Eden began to introduce ideas of the Arts and Crafts movement which would influence his work for the next decade, particularly in his work at Grace Church on-the-Hill. One such principle was that architecture should be a response to the needs of the society it was intended to serve; another was that the construction materials should be functionally expressive.

While apprenticing in the office of Strickland and Symons in 1887, Eden Smith had prepared a design for St. Simon's Church, Howard Street. In 1890 he person-

ally provided a design for a new church to the parish of St. Cyprian's, Seaton Village, an offshoot of the rapidly growing St. Thomas's Church, just to the east. Subsequent to his work at St. Thomas's, Smith went on to design many private residences in the Arts and Crafts idiom, including a picturesque grouping of irregularly planned but carefully detailed houses in the Wychwood Park neighborhood.

St. Thomas's Church is best experienced by taking part in one of the liturgical rites which marries worship with the building and music. Massive brick arcades support an exposed hammerbeam roof structure. Just outside these arcades, narrow passages provide access to the nave seats and then to the transept and the Lady Chapel. The windows are small except for those within the transepts.

It is one thing to convince a congregation that they should buy a new organ, and sometimes a more difficult thing to obtain approval for the removal of a carpet. St. Thomas' Church was successful both ways and made a great advance in 1991, both musically and acoustically. The organ is a large, eclectic instrument with attractive casework employing polished tin speaking principal pipes.

The Great Organ speaks into the south transept, the Choir into the choir area, and the Swell is double-decked in the north-east corner of the organ surrounded by Pedal pipes. Space on the gospel side of the chancel, formerly used for the enclosed Choir Organ, has been left free. Although the new organ has more pipes than the old one, it takes less space. All of the chests except for the lower Swell are electric-slider type. The treble pipes on slider chests are placed close together. The change from the old Pedal Open Wood flute 16′ to a Principal 16′ reduced the space needed for the Pedal Organ.

ORIGINS AND REVISIONS

1885 Samuel Warren organ built for the Sussex Avenue church.

1891 2-manual, 23 stop S. R. Warren organ built in the present church, an attached console on the epistle side.

1911 Casavant Organ Opus 459 installed, 3 manuals, 40 stops, enclosed Choir and console on the gospel side.

1955 New Casavant 3-manual console and 5 new stops installed.

1991 Guilbaut-Thérien electrified console and rebuilt organ with 60% new pipes and new windchests and casework.

Guilbault-Thérien, Inc., Opus 37, 1991, rebuild of Casavant 1911, S. R. Warren 1885

GREAT ORGAN		FEET	PIPES
1*	Violone	16	61
2	Principal	8	61
3*	Geigen	8	61
4	Flûte Harmonique	8	61
5	Bourdon	8	61
6	Octave	4	61
7†	Twelfth	2-2/3	61
8†	Fifteenth	2	61
9	Grande Fourniture III-IV		212
10	Fourniture	IV-V	na
11	Trompette	8	61
12	Clarion	4	61
13	Cornet V (prep.)	8	(solo)
14	Festival Trumpet (prep.)	8	(solo)

SWELL ORGAN (ENCLOSED)			
15†	Lieblich (ext # 20)	16	12
16*	Diapason	8	61
17*	Viola-da-Gamba	8	61
18*	Viola Celeste	8	61
19	Unda Maris II	8	110
20*	Rohrgedackt	8	61
21	Octave	4	61
22*	Chimney Flute	4	61

23	Nazard	2-2/3	61
24	Block Flute	2	61
25	Plein Jeu	III-IV	na
26	Double Trumpet	16	61
27	Trumpet	8	61
28*	Oboe	8	61
29†	Vox Humana	8	61
30	Clarion	4	61
	Tremulant		

CHOIR			
31	Spitz Principal	8	61
32	Cor de Nuit	8	61
33	Octave	4	61
34	Koppel Flute	4	61
35	Nazard	2-2/3	61
36	Lieblich Principal	2	61
37	Tierce	1-3/5	61
38	Octave	1	61
39	Plein Jeu	IV	244
40†	Clarinet	8	61
41	Rohr Schalmei	4	61
	Tremulant		
42	Cornet V (prep.)	8	(solo)
43	Festival Trumpet (prep.)	8	(solo)

(Continued overleaf)

SAINT TIMOTHY'S, NORTH TORONTO

100 Old Orchard Grove
Keates Organ Company Limited, 1954, additions 1993

St. Thomas's Church
(*Continued from page 127*)

PEDAL ORGAN

44	Untersatz (elect. Prep)	32	—
45	Principal (ext #49)	16	12
46	Violone (from #1)	16	—
47	*Subbass	16	32
48	Lieblich (from #15)	16	—
49	Octave	8	32
50	Geigen (from #3)	8	—
51	Stopped Flute	8	32
52	Choralbass	4	32
53	Nachthorn	4	32
54	Recorder (ext #53)	2	12
55	Mixture	IV	98
56	Contra Bombarde (elect. prep.)	32	—
57	†Bombarde	16	32
57	Double Trumpet (from #26)	16	—
59	Trompette	8	32
60	Clarion (ext #59)	4	12
61	Rohr Schalmei (from #41)	4	—

COUPLERS   na

COMBINATION PISTONS
Solid State Logic, 16 levels

ACTION
Electric slider chests, Swell reeds
on Pitman chests

*Warren pipes
†Casavant pipes, where known

In 1930 a small group of Anglicans began worshipping in the kindergarten room of John Wanless School. Within a year they had purchased a building site and had constructed the portion of a new church facility which today is St. Timothy's parish hall. The corner stone for the Parish Hall is dated 1932.

The process of building the church began with the appointment of a Building Committee in 1944. It is not unusual for such a committee to begin its investigations by exploring the types of buildings which other congregations had been building in recent times. This is also an approach often taken by organ committees who are determining which organ builders should be given consideration for a new project. What was unusual is that the Building Committee was obviously so impressed with one church they visited that they contacted the architect, Mr. Bruce Brown of the firm Bruce Brown and Brisley Architects, and ordered up a second church almost identical in plan and in detail. The church copied was not of the same denominational roots but was none other than Islington United, featured elsewhere in this book.

Islington United was completed in 1949. The Church of St. Timothy was consecrated on November 15, 1951. Islington United was to have cost $161,500 but by the time of its completion this figure was reported to have doubled. Fund-raising materials produced by St. Timothy's congregation anticipated a project cost of

$223,840. Either the final figures for Islington United were not yet known or the Anglicans thought they could do more for less.

It was clear that this was a great step of faith for a congregation which had only existed for twenty years. Islington United's Gothic Revival structure was a third building for a congregation which had been established in 1843. In order to meet the financial demands of construction, the Rev. Henry H. Marsh announced to parishioners that "each evening, I will be in the Church from 6:00 p.m. to 10:00 p.m. to receive your offering for the Lord's House. Bring your gift to The House of Prayer. Kneel when you enter and ask for God's blessing upon the Clergy, the People and the Building. Then make your offering at the Sanctuary Steps."

The completed building is a testimony to his faith and tenacity and there are important lessons to be learned from this vignette of history, perhaps of use to organ committees.

The additions of 1993 to St. Timothy's organ were by Keates-Geissler. The Keates Organ Company, Ltd. was established by Bert Keates in 1945 in London, Ontario and came to notice by building a classic style, unenclosed Positif division for Grace Anglican Church, Brantford. It was in the days when Toronto's senior organists were still advocating enclosed Choir organs. The firm moved to Lucan, Ontario in 1950 and to Acton in 1961. Bert Keates retired to the west coast in 1971, and when Mr. Dieter Geissler became president the name changed to Keates-Geissler.

The unusual appearance of a Pedal to Choir Coupler came about after organist Ashley Tidy lost the use of his right leg following spinal surgery.

Of course there is nothing new under the sun. The organ built in 1772 by Jean-Esprit Isnard at St. Maximim-en-Var for the 16th century Basilica of St. Mary Magdalene has a division called the Résonance permanently coupled from the pedal to the third manual. Seven of the ten stops including flutes and trumpets at 16', 8' and 4' pitch can be played from either the pedal clavier or the third manual. In some modern, large mechanical-action organs, the Résonance has been revived to add powerful solo and pedal voices.

Keates Organ Company Limited, 1954, additions 1993

GREAT ORGAN		FEET	PIPES
1	Open Diapason	8	68
2	Hohl Flute	8	68
3	Gemshorn	8	68
4	Principal	4	68
5	Traverse Flute	4	68
6	Twelfth	2-2/3	68
7	Fifteenth	2	61
8	Mixture	III	183

SWELL ORGAN (ENCLOSED)			
9	Bourdon	16	68
10	Geigen Diapason	8	68
11	Stopped Diapason	8	68
12	Viola da Gamba	8	68
13	Voix Celeste Ten C	8	56
14	Aeoline	8	68
15	Violina	4	68
16	Rohr Flute	4	68
17	Piccolo	2	61
18*	Scharf	III	183
19	Trompette	8	68
20	Oboe	8	68
21*	Hautbois	4	68
	Tremulant		

CHOIR ORGAN (ENCLOSED)			
22	Violin Diapason	8	68
23	Dulciana	8	68
24	Gedeckt	8	68
25*	Vox Angelica	8	68
26	Flute Ouverte	4	68
27	Nazard	2-2/3	61
28	Flautino	2	61
29	Clarinet	8	68
	Tremulant		

PEDAL ORGAN			
30	Open Diapason	16	32
31	Bourdon	16	32
32	Gedeckt (from #9)	16	—
33	Octave (ext #30)	8	12
34	Bass flute (ext #31)	8	12
35	Choral Bass (ext #33)	4	12
36	Double Trompette (ext #36)	16	12

COUPLERS
Great, Swell, Choir to Pedal 8, 4
Swell, Choir to Great 16, 8, 4
Great to Great 16, 4
Swell to Swell 16, 4
Choir to Choir 16, 4
*Pedal to Choir 8 (1996)

COMBINATION PISTONS
(CAPTURE TYPE)
Great   1 2 3 4 5 6   Thumb
Swell   1 2 3 4 5 6   Thumb
Choir   1 2 3 4 5   Thumb
Pedal   1 2 3 4 5   Thumb
General 1 2 3 4 5 6 7 8 Toe
Great and Pedal combination control

*new 1993

TIMOTHY EATON MEMORIAL CHURCH

230 St. Clair Avenue West
Casavant Organ Opus 583, 1914
New console, 1952

The interior of Timothy Eaton Memorial Church (opposite) bears little resemblance to how it looked for the first 20 years of its life (above). To a large extent these changes were to satisfy Lady Eaton's desire for a liturgy and architectural framework with stronger associations to those of the Church of England which she experienced during her many visits to England with Sir John.

Timothy Eaton was a devout Methodist. In May 1909, his widow and his son, John Craig Eaton, (later to become Sir John), announced a gift of funds to build a new Methodist church in an area of Toronto known as "The Hill," soon to be known as Forest Hill Village. In 1910, the generosity was substantially increased with the transfer of the one-block frontage on St. Clair Avenue and a larger building fund. The family made no stipulations on the naming of the new church, but in 1911 the congregation chose Timothy Eaton Memorial Church in recognition of their patron.

The chosen architects for the new church, the Toronto firm of Wickson & Gregg, had built a reputation on their design of Classical and Georgian Revival homes. The choice of the firm is likely related to the fact that, at the time of the bequest, it was completing John Craig Eaton's own mansion on that part of the crest of the Escarpment near Walmer Road called "Ardwold." Unfortunately this house was demolished in 1936. The final design of the church was approved in September 1912. Mrs. Timothy Eaton laid the cornerstone on 28 August 1913, and on 20 December 1914 the church was dedicated.

The use of Gothic-style architecture, based on English cathedral architecture of the fifteenth century, was not as appropriate for Methodists as it was for Anglicans or Roman Catholics. For Timothy Eaton Memorial Church, Wickson & Gregg designed an interior which was the usual Methodist auditorium, T-shaped, focused on a pulpit set in front of a terraced choir-loft and an immense window designed by Robert McCausland based on Holman Hunt's "The Light of the World." There was no central aisle, and additional seating was provided in galleries at the rear of the nave and the east and west sides. The organ was placed at the gallery level to the east of the choir.

During her visits to England with Sir John, Lady Eaton became attracted to the pomp and ceremony of the Church of England. This interest in ritual grew after Sir John's death in 1922, and she introduced kneeling benches, produced by the Royal Needleworkers at St. Paul's Cathedral in London, a more ritualistic communion service, and vestments for the clergy which corresponded to the seasons of the

Christian year. In 1929, Lady Eaton asked the Board of Timothy Eaton Memorial Church whether they would include a processional and recessional by the choir in their order of service. This was difficult, due to the lack of a central aisle. To overcome this impediment, Lady Eaton proposed in 1936 that a chancel and central aisle

The south (main) façade of Timothy Eaton Memorial Church is a masterful composition of rough cut Credit Valley stone, Indiana Limestone detailing and majestic stained glass windows.

be added to the church as a memorial to her late husband. Renovations proceeded under W. L. Somerville of Toronto in association with Hardie Phillip of New York, and were completed for Christmas of 1938.

This is how we find the church today – a nave measuring 35.5 metres (117 feet) in length and just over 13.7 metres (45 feet) in width, extended by a chapel to the east. While the south gallery has remained unchanged, the east and west galleries were set behind arches with stained glass windows above. The chancel is equal in width to the nave and just over 19 metres (63 feet) in depth. It is generally spartan in its appointments, drawing the eye to the very "unprotestant" altar with its cross, candelabra and flowers, and the reinstalled McCausland window above. The ceiling over the chancel is a five-sided panelled vault which is sparingly decorated in brilliant colours.

It is the exterior of the church which is architecturally most successful. Thanks to the commodious site and an equally ample budget, the architects have been able to exploit the Gothic vocabulary to its fullest. Monumental walls of rough-finished Credit Valley stone are supported by great buttresses, and orna-mented by the elaborate use of stone tracery. At the south façade, along St. Clair Avenue West, two majestic traceried windows are framed by buttresses which support the gable and parapet of the façade. At the south-west corner, a tower rises 30 metres (100 feet) and houses a carillon of 21 bells.

In October 1963 Edwin D. Northrup of Casavant read through files eight inches thick and wrote to organist David Ouchterlony, expounding upon the background of the building of the organ, the consultants who influenced the design, and the architect who "seems to have gone his own sweet way as 'HE was designing a church

132

and (was) not an organ builder' – As things went along, the openings became smaller and more irregular and the preliminary plans were not followed. – the widest opening came on the gallery side. As a result, the gallery complained while the organist and Choir complained but for the opposite reason. For 26 months

there was a re-fusal to pay for the organ "until it was made right." The architect hired Ernest Skinner, who found the "workmanship fine and first class but the organ did not sound right." The builder engaged Professor G. R. Anderson of the University of Toronto who was pioneering the design of a machine that would measure reverberation. He found that the church auditorium had .4 seconds of reverberation, the organ chamber .6 seconds and the church basement 2.0 seconds. After a time Lady Eaton is quoted as saying, "This organ question has been very badly handled, the whole blame has been put on the organ builders and as far as I can see, there is none of their fault…. Mr. Wickson (architect) this organ is a gift from Sir John and myself, and I will take all responsibility."

Whereas T. J. Palmer and Colonel Dixon influenced the design of the St. Paul's, Bloor Street (Anglican) organ the year before, the Eaton organ was affected by

G. D. Atkinson. Northrup notes, "And so whereas the organ started out in life as a fairly French organ with anglicised names, it became quite British with considerable 'American' influence of the Hope-Jones variety. Actually the Toronto center had some very active proponents of the 'Revolution in Organ Building' and GDA was at the height of his influence and maintained it for many years."

The next revolution in organ-building, the years of the "Organ Reform" of the post WW II period, saw no tonal changes except for the addition of 2 mutation ranks in 1952, a Nazard and a Tierce for the Choir Organ. When the revisions proposed in 1989 were started, another reform movement was already well underway and the organ turned toward the French late-Romantic style in which it was first conceived. So the turnaround was complete and what started out as a near disaster became one of Toronto's more glorious venues for organ and choral music, with a reservation or two. In May 1938, the organist Thomas Crawford wrote to the Chairman of the Building Committee, Mr. W. Kettlewell, to express concern that there would be too much sound in the chancel and not enough power down the church to support the singing. He obtained advice from Sir Ernest MacMillan, Dr. Charles Peaker, Richard Tattersall, Fred Silvester and two local organ builders. Having closed off the transepts, there was little that could be done, so things went from one evil to a lesser evil, or, rather, a much lesser evil.

ORIGINS, REVISIONS AND ADDITIONS

1914 Casavant Organ Opus 583 of 4 manuals, 86 stops installed in north east transept of cruciform church.

1938 Organ moved to 2 new chambers, Swell, Choir, Solo/Bombarde and Pedal reeds in west loft, Great and Pedal in east loft.

1952 New 5 manual console installed, with minor additions and Solo and Bombarde Organs separated.

1962 Original 15 h.p. wooden Casavant blower replaced with new Spencer Turbine Blower, organ chest actions re-leathered.

1985 Remote electro-pneumatic key action relays and switching replaced with SSL electronics

1992 Remote electro-pneumatic combination machines replaced with SSL multi-level electronics.

1989-2001 Tonal redesign and conversion of Ventil chest action to Pitman action plan written and carried out in stages.

Casavant Organ, Opus 583, 1914, new console 1952

GREAT ORGAN w.p. 4″

		FEET	PIPES
1	Double Open Diapason	16	68
2	Open Diapason I new 1	8	68
3	Open Diapason II new 1	8	68
4	Doppel Flote	8	68
5	Tibia Minor	8	68
6	Salicional	8	68
7	Octave	4	68
8	Wald Flute	4	68
9	Principal new	4	68
10	Twelfth	2/3	68
11	Fifteenth new	2	61
12	Cornet Ten. C new	V	245
13	Grand fourniture new	II-IV	208
14	Fourniture new	IV-V	293
15	Contra trompette new t&s	16	68
16	Trompette new t&s	8	68
17	Clarion new t&s	4	68
	Harp (Sw)		
	Chimes (Echo)		

SWELL ORGAN (ENCLOSED) w.p. 6″

18	Gedackt	16	68
19	Open Diapason	8	68
20	Stopped Diapason	8	68
21	Salicional	8	68
22	Viola de gambe	8	68
23	Voix céleste Ten. C	8	56
24	Octave	4	68
25	Flauto Traverso	4	68
26	Nazard new	2-2/3	61
27	Octavin new	2	61
28	Tierce new	1-3/5	61
29	Piccolo	1	61
30	Plein jeu new	V	305
31	Basson new t&s	16	68
32	Trompette new t&s	8	68
33	Oboe	8	68
34	Vox humana	8	68
35	Clarion new t&s	4	68
	Tremulant		
	Harp		
	Chimes		

CHOIR ORGAN (ENCLOSED) w.p. 5″

36	Contra Salicional	16	68
37	Principal	8	68
38	Melodia	8	68
39	Gemshorn	8	68
40	Gemshorn céleste Ten C	8	56
41	Prestant new	4	68
42	Dolce Flute	4	68
43	Twelfth	2-2/3	68
44	Fifteenth new	2	61
45	Tierce	1-3/5	61
46	Nineteenth	1-1/3	61
47	Cymbale new	III	183
48	Contra Fagotto new t&s	16	68
49	Clarinet new t&s	8	68
	Tremulant		
	Harp (Sw)		
	Chimes (Echo)		

SOLO ORGAN (ENCLOSED) w.p. 12″

50	Gedackt	8	68
51	Viole d'orchestre	8	68
52	Viole céleste	8	68
53	Principal	4	68
54	Orchestral Flute	4	68
55	Flûte Harmonique new	2	61
56	Jeu de clochette new*	II	122
57	Cor Anglais	8	68
58	Orchestral Oboe	8	68
	Tremulant		
	Harp (Sw)		

BOMBARDE (ENCLOSED WITH SOLO) w.p. 12″

59	Flûte harmonique 13 - 61 new *	8	61
60	Violincello	8	61
61	Principal new*	4	61
62	Tuba Mirabilis new t&s*	8	61
63	Tuba Clarion new t&s*	4	61

Pedal Organ

64	Double Open Diapason (6 polyphones) (ext. # 66)	32	6
65	Open Diapason II	16	32
66	Open Diapason I	16	32
67	Open Diapason (from #1)	16	—
68	Violone	16	32
69	Bourdon	16	32
70	Salicional (from #36)	16	—
71	Gedackt (from #18)	16	—
72	Octave (ext #66)	8	12
73	Principal (from #1)	8	—
74	Cello (ext. #68)	8	12
75	Flute (ext. #69)	8	12
76	Salicet (from #36)	8	—
77	Octave new	4	32
78	Super Octave (ext. #72)	4	12
79	Choral Bass (new ext #77)	2	12
80	Harmonics new (12, 15, 19, 22)	IV	128
81	Bombardon	32	32
82	Trombone (ext. #81)	16	12
83	Basson (from #31)	16	—
84	Trumpet (ext. #82)	8	12
85	Clarion (ext. #84)	4	12

Echo Organ (enclosed)

86	Violin Diapason	8	68
87	Rohrflote	8	68
88	Dulciana	8	68
89	Echo Gamba	8	68
90	Vox Angelica	8	68
91	Lieblich Flote	4	68
92	Piccolo	2	61
93	Cromorne	8	68
94	Vox humana	8	68
	Tremulant		
	Chimes		

Echo Pedal

95	Gedackt	16	32

(new l=new languids,
new t&s=new tongues and
shallots, new*=after 1995)

Couplers (S.S.L. electronic coupling system)

(intra-manual couplers on drawknobs,
inter-manual couplers on rocker tablets)

Great, Swell, Choir, Solo, Bomb.to Ped. 8, 4
Echo to Pedal 8
Swell, Choir, Solo, Bomb. to Great 16, 8, 4
Bomb. to Solo 8
Echo to Great, Swell Choir 8
Swell, Solo, Bomb. to Choir 16, 8, 4
Solo to Swell 16, 8, 4
Great to Great 16, 4
Swell to Swell 16, 4
Choir to Choir 16, 4
Solo to Solo 16, 4
Bomb. to Bomb. 16, 4
Echo to Echo 16, 4
Echo ON
Echo ON Main OFF (rocking button in left key jaw)
All Swells to Swell-Pedal
Combination coupler, Great and Pedal

Adjustable Combination Pistons
(8 level memory, SSL electronics)

Great	1 2 3 4 5 6 7	Thumb
Swell	1 2 3 4 5 6 7	Thumb
Choir	1 2 3 4 5	Thumb
Solo	1 2 3	Thumb
Bombarde	1 2 3	Thumb
Echo	1 2 3	Thumb
Pedal	1 2 3 4 5 6 7	Thumb
Couplers	1 2 3 4	Thumb
Generals	1 2 3 4 5 6	Thumb and toe
	7 8 9 10 11 12	Toe

Adjuster
General Release

Reversible Pistons

Great to Pedal	Thumb and toe
Swell, Choir, Solo, Bomb. to Pedal	Thumb
Swell, Choir, Solo to Great	Thumb
Swell to Choir	Thumb
Mezzo Forte	Toe
(program each level)	
Full Organ	Toe
(program each level)	
All Swells to Swell	Toe

Action
Electro-pneumatic
Ventil converting to Pitman.

Analysis

	STOPS	RANKS	PIPES	REAL STOPS
Great	17	28	1691	17
Swell	18	22	1365	18
Choir	14	16	1034	14
Solo	9	10	659	9
Bomb.	5	5	305	5
Echo	10	10	637	10
Pedal	22	10	422	7
Totals	95	101	6113	80

135

YORKMINSTER PARK BAPTIST CHURCH

1585 Yonge Street
Casavant Organ Opus 1241, 1928

It is sometimes easy to forget that most of our great congregations have come from simple roots; and, given the brevity of Canadian (recorded) history, the seed of these testaments to faith was in many cases not planted so long ago.

The history of Yorkminster Park begins in March 1870 in a room on Yorkville Avenue where a Sunday school was opened by a few workers from the former Bond Street Baptist Church. In September of the same year, a small chapel was built on Scollard Avenue and became known as Yorkville Baptist Church. In 1882 the congregation retained architect E.J. Lennox, who had designed St. Paul's Church, Bloor Street, to design an unassuming brick church on the southeast corner of Bloor and North (now Bay) Streets. Accordingly, the congregation was renamed Bloor Street Baptist Church. It appears that the congregation outgrew this building, because Sunday evening services began to be held in the Uptown Theatre at Yonge and Bloor Streets beginning in 1920 until the current building was constructed in 1928. These services were often attended by congregations of 3000 and had a special appeal for young people and students.

When a site for a new church was selected on Yonge Street, a short distance north of St. Clair Avenue, the neighbourhood was in the midst of growth. While the name "Yorkminster" suggests the Cathedral and Metropolitan Church of St. Peter founded in 627 A.D. in York, England, usually called the York Minster, it was selected to maintain a link with the first chapel located in Yorkville. There is, however, built into the wall of the tower of Yorkminster Park Baptist Church, a stone which for more than

What do St. Michael's Cathedral and Yorkminster Park Baptist Church have in common? Built into both are fragments of stone from Britain's York Minster. At Yorkminster Park this link with the past has been built into the wall of the tower. At St. Michael's both a piece of stone from a pier and a piece of oak from the roof of the York Minster are reported to have been contained in a lead box and are set behind the foundation stone.

500 years formed one of the mullions of the choir clerestory windows of the ancient York Minster.

The addition of the word "Park" to the church's name dates from 1961, when Park Road Baptist Church was destroyed by fire. Rather than rebuilding, the congregation decided to join Yorkminster Baptist Church.

Yorkminster Park Baptist Church was built in a Modern Gothic style to a design by Messrs. George Moorehouse and King Architects. The fact that these same architects had completed a new church for the congregation of Christ Church, Deer Park, directly across Yonge Street from the new site, would have given the congregation some expectation of results.

The church seats 1700 worshippers – 1200 in the nave and a further 500 on three balconies, one in the rear and two in the transepts. Walls of Owen Sound limestone support a steel trussed roof structure, above the plaster ceiling, which provides a space unobstructed by columns. This was a practical solution, but the net result is that the room ends up looking squat in spite of the height of the plaster vaults. The large windows along the north and south walls of the nave are characteristic of the late Gothic. The tracery is carved from Indiana limestone and the original amber glass is gradually being replaced by stained glass.

At the front of the church in the east end, the organ chambers open to the room through openings which match the shape and stonework of the windows. The placement is ideal, since neither the recently installed expanded metal screening nor the acoustics of the room distort the magnificent tone colours of this instrument.

The contract for the organ, Casavant Opus 1241, was signed on the 18th of January, 1927 for an amount of $25,590.00. No payment was due until the organ was delivered in 1928 for completion by Easter of that year. Cash flow was no problem because in 1928 Casavant built about 64 organs. Most contemporary builders require the final payment the day the organ is finished and accepted. The organ was donated by the Lieutenant Governor of Ontario, The Hon. Albert Matthews.

The organ was played for over 30 years by organist D'Alton McLaughlin. A letter from Mr. Edwin Northrup to Lawrence Phelps at Casavant gives some background. "This church was built and the organ opened by Farnam (Lynnwood Farnam) while I was in University. It is the only time I ever heard him play. The congregation was built around Rev. W. A. Cameron, and began a decline when his successor came. Then Park burned (Park Road Baptist Church) and new money came in with some curious results among which were a new organist Doug Elliott and a new minister to come. Elliott took his Mus. Bac. at Toronto and his ACCO. He used to go down to Methuen every year and study with Biggs, Poister and the lot."

It was a condition of Douglas Elliott's taking the post that the organ be redone.

A year of planning ensued with Elliott, Phelps, Northrup, Jackson and Dr. Charles Peaker as consultant. The key to the puzzle in the huge organ loft was to use a raised area over the baptistry to build a new, low-pressure Great Organ with schwimmer wind, since reservoirs were no longer needed. The old Solo Organ

138

chests, the only Pitman action chests in the organ, had the wind pressure dropped from 15" to 3" and the pipes all changed to classic style, open toe type. The division became the Positiv Organ. The old Great Ventil chests were used for the new Great reeds and for augmenting the Pedal Organ. The same Great reed chest was later converted to Pitman stop action. The technique was refined over the years and used to convert many of the pre-1930 organs to Pitman action. All of the Yorkminster chests were eventually converted to Pitman action and schwimmers.

Of all the organ lofts in Toronto, the Yorkminster loft is the one mostly likely to have been toured by citizens of Toronto. School children, organists and organ tour participants can safely be conducted up the wide stair to the organ loft doors and through the instrument from one side to the other without danger to the pipes, actions or themselves. Everything is there to see – reservoirs, schwimmers, windchests, expression boxes, and pipes of all families and sizes. All of the small pipes are out of reach from the passageway. The polyphonic pipes described in the glossary can be seen and touched. Visitors are able to hold a hand in the wind stream and feel the flutter of the pulses in the wind. The mechanism that shortens the pipe to raise the pitch one semitone can be seen in action. Short, carefully guided forays can be made into the organs at Metropolitan United Church and Timothy Eaton Memorial Church, but, in general, organ interiors are the tuner's domain.

Revisions and additions

1928   Organ installed 4 manuals, 69 stops, 69 ranks.

1965   Major rebuild to 73 stops, 87 ranks, 5045 pipes, new Great Organ of 11 stops, 15 ranks flues, 3 new reeds, 31 new ranks of flue and reed pipes for Swell, Choir and Positiv, Pedal 32' reed re-voiced, old console revised, Opening recital Dec 14, Douglas Elliott.

1971   added Great Scharff IV new pipes and chest and old Deer Park United Church Gedackt 16' pipes.

1975   new console dedicated October 8, recital Catherine Palmer.

1976   added old St. Barnabas Gedackt 16 chest 75 stops, 93 ranks, 5582 pipes.

1985   converted Swell reed chest to schwimmers and Pitman action.

1985   converted Great reed chest to schwimmers and Pitman action, cleaned Great and Positiv Organs, dead lengthened Great reeds.

1986   converted Swell Main chests to schwimmers and Pitman action, dead lengthened 3 Swell reeds, 16-8-4', cleaned Swell Organ, re-leathered. distributors, re-covered Pedal reed reservoir

1987   converted Choir and Pedal Organ chests to schwimmers and Pitman action, re-leathered distributor, cleaned Choir Organ, moved Pedal chest.

1988   converted console to multi-level, solid-state combination action.

1989   installed Great Principal 16'- 8' new pipes and chest.

1989   installed Pedal Contrebasse 16' (wood) new pipes and chest.

1990   installed Swell Bourdon 16' new pipes and chest, moved 10-2/3" Quinte.

1991   installed Swell Fagott 16', full length, new pipes and chest.

1992   installed Trompeta Real 8' new pipes (horizontal) and chest.

Casavant Organ Opus 1241, 1928

Great Organ

		Feet	Pipes
1	Principal	16	61
2	Quintaton	16	61
3	Principal I	8	61
4	Principal II (ext #1)	8	12
5	Bourdon	8	61
6	Gemshorn	8	61
7	Octave	4	61
8	Spitzflote	4	61
9	Nazat	2-2/3	61
10	Superoctave	2	61
11	Blockflote	2	61
12	Sesquialtera II	2-2/3	122
13	Mixtur IV	1-1/3	244
14	Sharf IV	2/3	244
15	Bombarde	16	61
16	Trompette	8	61
17	Clarion	4	61
18	Trompeta Real	8	61
	Great Unison Off		
	Great 4' to Great		

Swell Organ (enclosed)

		Feet	Pipes
19	Bourdon	16	68
20	Open Diapason	8	68
21	Clarabella	8	68
22	Stopped Diapason	8	68
23	Viol de Gamba	8	68
24	Voix Celeste	8	68
25	Aeoline	8	68
26	Principal	4	68
27	Flauto Traverso	4	68
28	Fifteenth	2	61
29	Cornet I - II	2-2/3	110
30	Fourniture IV	2	244
31	Cymbal IV	1	244
32	Double Trumpet	16	68
33	Contra Fagott	16	68
34	Trumpet	8	68
35	Oboe	8	68
36	Vox Humana	8	68
37	Clarion	4	61
	Tremulant		
	Swell 16' to Swell		
	Swell Unison Off		
	Swell 4' to Swell		
	Trompeta Real	8	

Choir Organ (enclosed)

		Feet	Pipes
38	Contra Gamba	16	68
39	Salicional	8	68
40	Rohrflote	8	68
41	Flauto Dolce	8	68
42	Flute Celeste	8	68
43	Principal	4	68
44	Lieblichflote	4	68
45	Nazard	2-2/3	61
46	Piccolo	2	61
47	Tierce	1-3/5	61
48	Petite Mixture IV	2/3	244
49	Basson (1/2 length)	16	61
50	Basson (ext #49)	8	12
51	Clarinet	8	68
52	Cor Anglais	8	68
	Tremulant		
	Choir 16' to Choir		
	Choir Unison Off		
	Choir 4' to Choir		
	Trompeta Real	8	

Positiv Organ

		Feet	Pipes
53	Nason Gedackt	8	61
54	Violflote	8	61
55	Principal	4	61
56	Koppelflote	4	61
57	Doublette	2	61
58	Hohlflote	2	61
59	Quintflote (GG)	1-1/3	54
60	Sifflote	1	61
61	Zimbel IV	1/4	244
62	Krummhorn	8	61
	Tremulant		
	Positif 16' to Positif		
	Positif Unison Off		
	Positif 4' to Positif		
	Trompeta Real	8	

Pedal Organ

		Feet	Pipes
63	Double Open Wood (6 polyphonic)	32	26
64	Open Wood (ext #63)	16	12
65	Contrebasse (wood)	16	32
66	Principal	16	32
67	Violone	16	32
68	Bourdon	16	32
69	Contra Gamba (from #38)	16	—
70	Quintaton (from #2)	16	—
71	Gedackt	16	32
72	Quint	10-2/3	32
73	Octave	8	32
74	Bourdon (ext #68)	8	12
75	Dulciana	8	32
76	Choral Bass	4	32
77	Flute	4	32
78	Blockflote	2	32
79	Rauschquint III	5-1/3	96
80	Mixture V	2-2/3	160
81	Bombardon	32	32
82	Bombarde (ext #81)	16	12
83	Basson (from #49)	16	—
84	Trumpet (ext #82)	8	12
85	Basson (from #49)	8	—
86	Clarion	4	32
87	Basson (from #49)	4	—
	Trompeta Real (from #18)	8	—

Couplers

Manuals to pedal 8', 4'
Manuals to manuals 16', 8', 4'
Pedal pistons on
Great pistons
Balanced Pedals
Swell and Choir
expression
Crescendo

Adjustable Pistons and Accessories

Solid State Logic combination
system 24 levels
Programable list system.
Generals - 12 thumb and
toe pistons
Pedal - 8 thumb and toe pistons
Great, Swell, Choir 8 thumb
pistons
Positif 6 thumb pistons
Full Organ on each level
Crescendo A B C adjustable
Lock on each level
General cancel piston

Analysis of 1927 Organ

	Stops	Ranks	Pipes	Real Stops
Great	16	20	1346	16
Swell	17	23	1625	17
Choir	13	13	793	13
Solo	9	9	612	9
Pedal	14	7	302	7
Totals	69	72	4678	62

Analysis of 1994 Rebuilt Organ

	Stops	Ranks	Pipes	Real Stops
Great	18	24	1476	17
Swell	20	23	1672	19
Choir	16	17	1112	14
Positif	10	12	725	9
Pedal	26	20	746	16
Totals	90	99	5731	75

140

Appendix

Glossary of organ terms

Acoustic

The aspect of acoustics which is of most concern to church and concert hall organists and choirs is the *reverberation time* which is the length of time it takes for sound to die away measured in decibels and seconds. A sound level meter is used for professional measurements. If the reverberation time is 2.5 seconds or more it is going to be good for church music. Three typical examples of Toronto churches measured by Klepper Marshall King Associates Ltd. gave for St. Andrew's Presbyterian Church 1.7 seconds at 500 cycles empty and 1.0 seconds with the congregation present. For St. Andrew's United Church, Bloor Street it was 1.2 seconds at 500 cycles, empty or full. St. Michael's Cathedral just makes it with 3.2 seconds empty and 2.3 seconds full at 500 cycles. *Surround* refers to the sensation among the congregation that they are not alone and the air around them is full of supporting sound, either direct from others or reflected. Also important is *fall-off*, the way the sound level reduces as it is heard down the church. There are at least 18 different qualities for gauging acoustics. Reverberation time is the most important. Very few Toronto churches make the grade.

Compound stops

These are similar to *mixtures* but contain pitches other than the unison and quints. The cornet is the most common. It always includes the interval of the sixth and uses pipes of flute tone. The Sesquialtera is the same but uses pipes of principal tone. If the Cornet has five ranks the pitches are at 8', 4', 2-2/3', 2' and 1-3/5'. If it has two ranks they are 2-2/3' and 1-3/5'.

Cone tuning

The old way to tune small, metal flue pipes was (is) to open or close the tops of the pipes with tuning cones. Flared out, the pipe is sharpened and coned inward it is flattened. The tuner's tool is a double ended brass *tuning cone*, tapered to a point at one end and cone shaped at the other. The advantage is that once tuned, it is hard for animals or intruders in the organ to knock the pipes out

A demonstration of 'sleeve tuning' in the new Great Organ at Yorkminster Park Baptist Church when Alan Jackson was about 40. The pipework is 'open toe'. The spotted metal of which the pipes were made is about 55% tin and 45% lead. The 'rank' being tuned is the Octave 4', the longest pipe having a speaking length of four feet. It is the stop used to set the temperament and from which most of the other pipes in the division will be tuned. Tuning the four rank mixture in the foreground requires mutes so that three of the pipes can be silenced while the fourth is tuned.

A demonstration of 'cone tuning' at the Eaton 'voicing jack' when Alan Jackson was about 30.

of tune. The disadvantages are many. To start with, it takes a great deal of skill to cut the pipe just enough so that after it is voiced for the final time in the church, the top is slightly coned inward and in fine tune. If the consultant decided later that the stop was too soft, or if the pitch of the division changed and had to be lowered, the pipes would have to be made again or lengthened. The very act of tapping the pipes on the top sometimes lowers

the height of the mouth and upsets the voicing. Years of tuning can seriously change the voicing. Coning tends to make the pipes too tight in the racks so they flatten and need even more tuning.

CONTINUO ORGAN OR PORTATIVE ORGAN

This is an organ, small enough to be portable which can be placed on a stage or amongst a choir or instruments to play the basso

continuo of a composition marked with figures to indicate the harmonies to be played on a keyboard instrument. Most commonly it is the solo recitatives and arias of early music for which this instrument is needed. There is a good deal of music for one manual which can be played on a continuo organ of 4 or 5 stops.

(Above and left) The Klaus Becker portative organ used to accompany the choir in the chancel of Deer Park United Church has flue stops at 8', 4' and 2' and a reed at 8' pitch.

(Left, bottom) The Continuo or Portative Organ by Orgues Létourneau built in 1990 contains four ranks of pipes.

The Orgues Létourneau Portative Organ Opus 29, built for Christopher Dawes in 1990, is such an organ. It has 4 stops, a Gedeckt 8', Holtz Flöte 4', Principal 2' and Quinte 1 1/3' (1-12 at 2/3'). The single manual compass is of 51 notes from CC to d''. The organ resides at St. James' Cathedral but is moved from place to place to accompany various early and modern music ensembles.

COUPLER

A device used to join together the key action of two or more keyboards, including manuals to pedalboard. A Super coupler or Coupler 4' joins them an octave higher and a Sub coupler, an octave below. In tracker organs, coupling increases the pressure on the keys so couplers are adjusted to connect a little late so that two or more pallets do not have to be plucked open at one time. This is called *stagger*. In large tracker organs, electric couplers are sometimes used. For tubular pneumatic action organs, little circular cells with in and out channels and a disc of lambskin controls the coupling. Passage of air through the cell is controlled by the coupler stop action, which charges or discharges the channel common to all the cells. For electric or electro pneumatic action organs, the coupling is controlled with gang switches or, for solid state electronic systems, with transistors.

Cypher (cipher)

The unwanted sounding of a note or pipe when no key is depressed. The possible causes are too numerous to mention ranging from a leak in the roof to a moth cocoon in a magnet cap.

Direct electric action

A few (very few) builders use direct electric action to open the pipe valves of a wind chest. Usually, a felt and leather disc is mounted on a soft iron armature bent in a hook shape. The tip of the hook is attracted to one pole of an electro magnet. A coil spring holds the pallet closed. The only advantage of direct electric action is that construction is simple and it allows for unification of the ranks. Among the disadvantages is the fact that the iron armature is heavy and liable to cause the pallet to bounce open after closing. Repeated chords then say but-a but-a but-a. Sometimes a metal chip gets caught in the gap at the magnet pole and causes a cypher. Sometimes the hinges corrode and stick or the hinge wears and the hook touches the pole and sticks. Each magnet draws up to 1/3 of an ampere so that playing all the stops draws huge amounts of current. Direct electric magnets are used for the pull-downs for electric slider chests but one magnet only is needed for each note of the scale as compared with 10 magnets in a 10 stop direct action chest.

Electro-pneumatic action

Organs operated by electro-pneumatic action use electric contacts at the keyboards and cables to the windchests to play the notes. Low voltage, usually 12 volts DC, arriving at the windchest powers a small horseshoe magnet containing an iron disc, which is pulled away from a port to exhaust the air pressure in a channel connected to a pouch of thin lambskin. The motion moves a valve which exhausts a key channel, which runs across the windchest and connects with the pneumatics, usually pouches, for the pipe valves. The stop action for electro-pneumatic action can be Pitman type or Ventil.

Equal temperament

Only a handful of Toronto organs are not tuned in equal temperament. The Knox College organ is the best known example of unequal temperament and uses a form of mean tone. Equal temperament allows one to play in all the keys without running into any wildly out of tune chords. In equal temperament, all the fifths are a little out of tune, the fourths beat a little faster and the thirds beat horribly fast. Modern ears have become accustomed to the wide thirds but the sustained tones of an organ accentuate the problem. Mixing tempered mutations with natural mutations does not help. Some 18th century builders used to build organs with one set of pipes for E flat and another for D sharp. Similarly for F sharp and G flat. They could enjoy the peaceful sound of pure thirds and calm mixtures. An organ with a number of sub semitones was built for Houghten Chapel, Wellesley College in Massachusetts in 1981 by Charles Fisk. To choose between one or the other semi tone the player plays on the front or the back of the black note. Needless to say, most organists have enough to contend with without having to decide which end of the key to press. Evidence of the split semitones of the early days was found in the wealthy towns, such as Lübeck, where the most accomplished organists would have played.

Expression box

The enclosure which allows the organist to reduce the volume of sound from any one division of the organ is sometimes called the *Swell box* (for the Swell) or *Choir box* etc. It is generally conceded that control is best when the expression pedal at the console is mechanically attached to the shutters that swing open or closed as desired. Large organs need large boxes with many shutters and the larger the box is, the thicker the walls and shutters must be to contain the sound. Vertical shutters standing on steel pins rotate very easily and are generally used. If mechanical connection is not possible, expression engines are used, generally electro-pneumatically operated with a number of accordions or pneumatics operating on high wind pressure. The number of motions may range from 5 in small organs to 16 for large motors. Large, Romantic organs as at Metropolitan United Church need very powerful, fast acting engines. Classic style organs as at Our Lady of Sorrows Church have no expressive divisions at all. Expression boxes were not invented until the end of the eighteenth century.

Fall-off (see Acoustic)

Flue pipe

Organ pipes are either flues or reeds. Flues are like whistles and produce a tone by forming a wind sheet which contains eddies of air which are caught by the upper lip of the pipe mouth to excite the body or resonator into vibration at pitches determined by the length of the resonator. If made of metal, the metal used is a mixture of tin and lead, more tin for brightness in principals and strings and more lead for flutes. If made of wood, they are often of oak and for large pedal pipes of whitewood or pine.

MECHANICAL (KEY) ACTION

Called *tracker* action just as often, mechanical key action implies that the keys at the organ console are connected to the pallets in the wind chests which admit wind to the pipes. The trackers are long strips of wood about 1 mm thick by about 8 mm wide. They can pull (and push a little bit) for considerable distances vertically (25 feet to the Oberwerk in Deer Park United) but do not function well horizontally because they do not lie straight without support or *hangers* (Our Lady of Sorrows Great Organ). Some builders use wire trackers and a system for keeping them under tension (Roy Thomson Hall). If well-built, the suction of opening and closing of the pallets can be sensed at the surface of the key action.

MIXTURE

This is what remains of the Blockwerk when all the stops on a chest were played together. Once it was possible to separate the useful lower pitch stops to play them separately, the remaining two, three or four ranks played together and furnished the brilliance. *Fourniture* is the French name. They call the very top ranks the *Cymbale*. Most mixture stops are made up of principal toned pipes speaking as unisons and octaves and ranks at the fifth. The tierce or seventeenth is occasionally used as in the Metropolitan United organ and the Knox College organ. The ranks rarely continue at one pitch from bass to treble. The ranks are made to 'break' back to lower pitches. The result is to brighten and clear the bass end and to deepen and fortify the treble. Note that playing a single note with a Mixture IV drawn causes four pipes to play.

MUTATIONS

Organ stops which play at a pitch other than the normal pitch or some octave or octaves above or below normal pitch are mutations. Any one of the natural series of overtones could be used. Over-blow a C pipe and it first speaks an octave above which is not a mutation. Blow harder and it speaks a G a twelfth above which is a mutation. Blowing even harder it plays a C, not a mutation but next it blows an E which is a mutation. The mutations in a listed specification are easily recognized. The Nazard is usually at 2-2/3', the Tierce at 1-3/5' and the Quint at 1-1/3. These are the most common ones.

OPEN TOE (VOICING)

With the Organ Reform Movement came the revival of a method of making and voicing flue pipes that forced even the most experienced voicers to re-learn their trade. For a century and a half or more, voicers had been making the job easy by nicking the languids of the flue pipes and doing all the changes in volume by opening or closing the toes of the pipes. Now the toes were to be made wide open on all flutes and most principals. Nicks were not allowed unless they could not be seen. The volume was controlled by the width of the flue. Paper-thin steel tools were used to open the flues and tiny hammers used to close them. Adjustments of attack and brightness became very tricky and precise. Pipes sizzled and chiffed and took on a rich timbre and spoke more softly and clearly. By the mid 1970s toes were being closed a little and a more moderate style evolved. Pipes still chiffed and had a good attack but the noises did not detract from the music.

PEDALBOARD

This word, not in the dictionary, refers to the keyboard played by the organist's feet. The modern pedalboard has 32 notes, from CC corresponding to c two octaves below middle c, to g above middle c. Standard measurements were set by the American Guild of Organists and agreed to by the RCCO which determine the radius of the vertical concavity and the radius of the splay of the keys which are close together at the back and spread at the front, all meant to follow the arc of the organist's feet and to avoid awkward reaching for top and bottom notes. The old pedalboards as at St. Paul's Basilica, Power Street, were flat on the floor. The sharp keys at St. Paul's are made longer at the treble and bass. This pedalboard has 30 notes. Earlier ones had 27. The Mead Organ at St. Clement's has just one octave. Builders of historic replica organs still make flat pedalboards. Touring organists often find them in use on the old organs of Europe and America too.

PISTONS

To an organist, a piston is a button mounted under the keys of the manuals or along the front of the pedalboard which when depressed, causes the stops to go on or off, depending on how the pistons have been set. In early days the combinations were set by the builder as at St. Michael's Cathedral and a toe lever moved the drawstops, sliders and all. Later consoles were provided with mechanisms that could be toggled on or off either by holding the piston and forcing the stops (*hold-set*) or by holding a setter button that put the system in setting mode while the piston was pushed (*capture type*). As soon as electronic memory systems were invented, the way was opened to simplify and expand the possibilities to include any number of 'memory levels' at low cost.

A view of the back of the Canadian Pipe Organ Co. console at St. Anthony's R. C. Church showing the tubing made of a mixture of lead and tin which carries the message from the keys, under the floor and to the windchests in the organ loft. The few electric wires are for the electro-pneumatic piston action.

The recitalist playing on a Saturday night could use a dozen levels, one per piece, play the concert with no pause for resetting between numbers, and still not disturb the combination prepared by the organist for Sunday morning. The organist may have set half a dozen levels for regular use, each ready for the style of a different composer.

Pitman chest

Pitman action was invented either by the British or the Americans just prior to 1900. It is a type of stop action that uses a small disc of leather to block or open the air channel leading to the pneumatic for the valve which admits air to any one pipe or group of pipes (in the case of a mixture stop). It is favoured because of the speed and simplicity and for the fact that universal wind is possible.

Pneumatic Action

With air under pressure available for blowing organ pipes it stands to reason that someone would decide to make use of air power to move things. Early in the 19th century, organ builders were using pneumatic power to open valves for organ pipes set at some distance from the main windchests. In 1836 Thomas Barker took out a French patent for the 'Barker lever,' a mechanism which used long, hinged pneumatics to assist the opening of the pallets of tracker organ windchests. The invention was used extensively in the large organs of Cavaillé-Coll and other European builders. The next stage in the use of pneumatic action was the tubular pneumatic organ which employed lead tubing, in place of trackers, to connect the keys of the organ console to the pipe valves in the windchests. This is the type of action used for organs at St. Anthony's Church, Toronto, and at St. Cecilia's Church described on page 94.

Polyphone

The organs at Convocation Hall, St. Paul's Bloor Street, Timothy Eaton Memorial Church and Yorkminster Park Baptist Church each list in the Pedal Organ a number of polyphonic pipes. At Yorkminster, for example, there are 32 keys on the pedalboard but only 26 pipes in the rank. The builder has provided the six largest pipes with large flaps or pallets, hinged and connected to long rods and a special action in the wind chest. If the organist plays bottom CCCC of the Pedal Double Open Wood 32' the pipe speaks that pitch. Playing CCCC# causes the flap to open while the same CCCC pipe continues to play but is sharpened one semitone. Low DDDD, EEEE, FFFF# and GGGG# and AAAA# do the same. The saving in material, space and cost is enormous.

Rank

A row or set of pipes, one for each key of the keyboard. One pipe gives one note of one tone and one pitch. If there are 61 notes on the keyboard then there will be 61 pipes for one rank. The pedalboard may have 32 keys, so a rank will contain 32 pipes.

Reed pipes

Reed pipes always have a curved tongue of brass or bronze. Stops are occasionally made with free reeds in the manner of harmonica and harmonium reeds, but most are beating reeds which vibrate against the flattened opening of the brass shallot. The shape and dimension of the shallot has a considerable effect on the tone of the pipe but the resonator determines the character, whether it is a trumpet, oboe or clarinet. A simple cone produces trumpet tone. A slender taper with a bell on top makes an oboe. A cylindrical, parallel resonator makes a clarinet. Every imaginable shape of resonator has been used, everything from match boxes to round apples. It is the reeds that continually need tuning and that is partly because the tuning is affected by dirt getting trapped under the tongues. Other times they are tuned because they are tunable. When the temperature rises, flue pipes go sharp and reeds go flat or stay about the same pitch. Reeds can be tuned quickly and easily using the springs that rest on the tail of the tongues. Flues will stand in tune for five or ten years, and they return to the pitch they were tuned at whenever the temperature also returns to where it was.

RESERVOIR
As the name implies the organ reservoir holds the wind needed to play the pipes. They are usually rectangular wood 'boxes' with a *top* made with a thick wooden frame with access panels screwed on top. A *gate* in the form of a roller blind or a disc moves with the motion of the top and admits air, replacing that consumed by the pipes. Springs or weights press downward on the top to set the wind pressure.

RESULTANT
Many organs, as for example the Casavant Organ at Grace Church on-the-Hill, obtain a 32' effect from the Pedal flues by combining a pipe at 16' pitch with a second pipe at 10 2/3' pitch, which is to say, one fifth above the unison 16'. Everywhere in the organ, in fact, pipes sounding one fifth apart generate the octave below the unison. Mixture stops of quints and unisons use this 'resulting pitch' to impart gravity to the sound of the principal chorus. In the pedal organ, the Resultant represents a saving in space and cost. In small churches which are too short to allow the long standing waves of 32' notes to form, resultant stops may work better than real 32' pipes. Note that, at Lawrence Park Community Church and at St. Andrew's Evangelical Lutheran Church, the resultant pitch is wired from other existing ranks. At Grace Church, a special octave of 12 stopped quint pipes has been built to generate the notes.

SEQUENCER (OR SEQUENCE RECORDER)
This computer software or hardware unit can be used with any MIDI (Musical Instrument Digital Interface) equipped organ. It memorizes and plays back MIDI messages and Control Changes and stores them along with timing information. It allows an organist to record a performance and play it back and also to edit the performance. When MIDI ports are installed the organ can be used to play synthesized sounds and can be connected to make use of computer music notation software. There is also the possibility of connecting portable keyboards to play the organ from various locations in the room including the organ loft.

SCHWIMMER
Schwimmer winding was available in the 19th century but little used because it was not applicable to Ventil windchests. It requires universal wind and uses a floating panel, usually forming part of the underside of the windchest. The panel is connected to rigid, pivoted bars or rods which hold an intake valve over the wind supply pipe. Any slight motion of the floating panel with the drawing of wind by the pipes, opens the valve and controls the flow of wind into the chest. This differs from reservoir winding where the reservoirs control the volume of air needed. Schwimmer wind is very stable and eliminates wind shake completely. Builders of historical organs call it *hard wind* and do not often use it. Others call it *buoyant* and liken it to a singer with good breath pressure. Schwimmers conserve space and are simple to recover. In order to produce a tremulant effect it is usual to mount a pneumatic and action to push and pull on the schwimmer table. A fan tremolo can also be used. Two or four broad blades of light material are made to revolve on a shaft driven by a motor and the assembly is hung above the pipes. D. W. Karn organs, which often had universal chests and a form of schwimmer wind, had fan tremolos driven pneumatically by a set of three folding pneumatics with valves. Motors of this type drive the player organs built by Aeolian.

SLIDER CHEST
More correctly, a slider and pallet chest is the windchest used for mechanical action organs. In the lower part of the chest is a plenum holding the wind which is fed into key channels, one per note on the keyboard. Depressing a key pulls open a long, narrow pallet which fills one of the key channels running across the width of the chest. Running the length of the chest are the *sliders* which are long strips of wood or plastic bored with holes which line up with the key channels below and the pipe holes above. Modern sliders are usually made of plastic with a fibre core. Circular seals are used to make an airtight joint against the moving slider. In the old organs with wooden sliders the air did

leak but was carried away by shallow channels cut into the table top. The advantage of the slider chest, aside from providing the all-important pluck of the key action, is that all pipes for one note receive air from one pallet. The problem arises when the one pallet may not be able to supply enough wind to play all the pipes when the organist pulls out all the stops. This causes high pitched pipes to drop out of tune.

If the chest is not connected to the keyboards by trackers but is operated by electric pull-downs, it is called an *electric slider chest.* These are sometimes used to save space. Without the need for a circular pouch under every pipe, the treble pipes can be placed much more closely together.

Slider or sleeve tuning

Cylindrical flue pipes in most organs are tuned with tuning slides or sleeves, short cylinders of aluminum or plated iron, lightly sprung around the top of each pipe so that the tuner can tap the slide up to make the pitch flatter or down to shorten the pipe and make it sharper. The advantage of sleeve tuning is that any amount of tuning does not harm the pipes and pitch changes are no problem. The disadvantage is that birds, squirrels and organists can knock the pipes out of tune.

Stop

An organ stop may be turned on or off by pulling a drawknob, tilting a tablet or depressing a tab. What is controlled by the stop may be a single rank of pipes of a particular tone and pitch or it may control two or more ranks of pipes of a mixture. A stop may bring on a sound by switching into the pipes and action to play the pipes of another stop in which case there may be no pipes belonging to that stop. Originally, all the ranks on a windchest spoke together until a method was devised to run a slider under one rank of pipes and *stop* it from playing. This is the origin of the word as used in organ terminology. Eventually all the ranks had sliders to turn them on and off except for higher pitched ranks would be left together in groups of two, three or more ranks to speak as mixtures.

Straight organ

If an organ is not a unit organ, it is a straight organ.

Surround (see Acoustic)

Suspended action

A method of building mechanical key action which uses long keys pivoted at the very back end of each key. The pull-down or tracker is attached just behind the key desk and runs straight up to the pallet in the wind chest or through a roller to the pallet. It is a good way to play a large number of stops and works for organs built vertically. The leverage is not needed for small divisions and the inertia of the extra long keys can spoil repetition. Most tracker organs use a key hinged in the middle. The tail of the key pushes up on a *sticker* or pulls upward a wire fitted with collars to engage the levers of the various couplers.

Tracker action (see mechanical action)

Unit organ

With the coming of electric pneumatic action organs it became possible to make each pipe on a windchest play independently. Why not then take one rank of pipes and play it an octave higher and an octave lower and at the fifth etc. etc.? The ultimate unit organ was the "Hope-Jones Unit Orchestra" built as the Wurlitzer Theatre organ. The Diapason 8' rank used 61 pipes from CC 8 to c61. Using switches and relays and 24 more treble pipes, the tone was extended to 4' and to 2' pitch. Below CC 8' were added 24 Diaphones, a type of reed stop with circular discs on a flat spring beating against an opening leading to tapered wood resonators. The lower octave of this stop used at Shea's Theatre, Toronto was installed behind and outside the concrete chamber on the right hand side. The longest pipe, 32' high was mitred, with the top aimed across the ceiling of the theatre.

Unit organs went out of popularity after the Organ Reform but have returned with some differences. Mutations are no longer borrowed from unison ranks and independent mixtures are added. The organs sound in tune where they did not when mutations were being borrowed from unison ranks. It has been possible to compete well, price wise with electronic organs by using the unit system.

Universal chest

If a chest is not divided into cells, as in a Ventil chest, then the wind 'goes everywhere'. For these chests the stop action controls the off and on mode by some method other than removing the supply of wind. Pitman and unit chests use universal wind.

Ventil chest

In a Ventil chest the stops are turned on and off by charging or discharging the air pressure in a cell below the ranks of pipes. The windchest is therefore divided the long way, one cell per stop and air is admitted to each cell by a large valve controlled by a smaller secondary valve controlled by a still smaller primary valve tripped by an electric chest magnet or in pneumatic action organs, by a lead tube. The advantage of Ventil action is that in the event of a cypher on one pipe, the pipe can be silenced by putting the stop off. The disadvantages are that the stops are slow going on and off and can be noisy. When a stop is off, the air pressure in the key action channels causes the pneumatics in chests using pouches to balloon. In time the lambskin takes a rounded form, develops a knuckle action and becomes slow and does too much bending at the rim causing it to break prematurely.

Water motor

A device for operating the feeders which supply air under pressure for organ reservoirs. A double-acting, hydraulic cylinder fed and exhausted by a valve is connected to a lever and driven up and down doing work similar to what the organ pumper did by hand. Water motors were promoted in the Toronto area in the mid and late 19th century by S. R. Warren who supplied them to St. Michael's Cathedral, St. James Cathedral and the Church of St. George the Martyr.

Photo credits

149

All photography by Brian J. Thompson unless noted as below:

Bibliography

150

Armstrong, Frederick H., *A City in the Making, Progress, People & Perils in Victorian Toronto*, Dundurn Press, 1988.

Arthur, Eric, *Toronto, No Mean City,* University of Toronto Press, 1964, revised by Otto, Stephen, 1986.

Careless, J. M. S., *Toronto, An Illustrated History to 1918*, James Lorimer & Company, 1984.

Careless, J. M. S., *Toronto, An Illustrated History since 1918*, James Lorimer & Company, 1985.

Cooke, William ed. *The Parish and Cathedral of St. James'*, Toronto 1797-1997, 1998.

Dendy, William and Kilbourne, William, *Toronto Observed, Its Architecture, Patrons, and History*, Oxford University Press, 1986.

Dendy, William, *Lost Toronto*, McCelland & Steward, 1993.

Duff, Daniel S., ed. *The St. James-Bond Story*, 1983.

Edmondson, Ernest, *A History of Sherbourne Street*, Carlton Printers, 1993.

Encyclopedia of Music in Canada, ed. Kallmann, Potvin, Winters, 1981.

Graham, Audrey: *150 Years at St. John's York Mills*, 1966.

Greif, David, *In the Fullness of Time, A History of the Church of Saint Mary Magdalene*, Toronto, Coach House Press, 1990.

Harman & Upshall, H. M. & W. G. *The Story of the Church of St. George the Martyr of Toronto*, 1945.

Iglauer, Edith, *Seven Stones, A Portrait of Arthur Erickson Architect*, Harbour Publishing/University of Washington Press, 1981.

Kalman, Harold, *A History of Canadian Architecture*, Oxford University Press, 1994.

Laycock, Margaret and Myrvold, Barbara, *Parkdale in Pictures, Its Development to 1889*, Toronto Public Library Board (Local History Handbook No. 7), 1991.

Laycock, Margaret and Myrvold, Barbara, *Danforth in Pictures,* Toronto Public Library Board (Local History Handbook No. 3), 1992.

Lewis, Joyce C. *Chronicles of the Church of St. Clement, Eglinton: 1891 – 1991*, 1991.

Litvak, Marilyn M., *Edward James Lennox, Builder of Toronto*, Dundurn Press, 1995.

Lundell, Liz, *The Estates of Old Toronto*, The Boston Mills Press, 1997.

MacRae, Marion and Adamson, Anthony, *Hallowed Walls: Church Architecture in Upper Canada*, Clarke, Irwin & Company Limited, 1975.

Marchetto, Fr. Ezia, *A Vision Shared, The Fresco at Saint Anthony's Church*, The Basilian Press, 1998.

McHugh, Patricia, *Toronto Architecture, a City Guide*, McClelland & Stewart Inc., second edition, 1989.

Moon, Lynda, Myrvold, Barbara and Ridler, Elizabeth, *Historical Walking Tour of Lawrence Park*, Toronto Public Library Board in Cooperation with the North Toronto Historical Society, 1994.

Robertson, John Ross, *Landmarks of Toronto*, 1904.

Tate, C. Ian P., *The Church of the Holy Trinity*, 1965.

The authors

ALAN T. JACKSON

Alan Jackson was born in Toronto in 1926 and spent his youthful years tinkering in his fathers basement workshop. Upstairs were 2 reed organs on which he not only learned to play the organ but also about their mechanics while dismantling them! In 1945 he became assistant organist at the Church of the Transfiguration, and St. Simon the Apostle, then was organist and choirmaster at Little Trinity, All Hallows, Church of George the Martyr, St. Stephen's, Beverley Hills and at St. Hilda's, Fairbank.

A summer job in July of 1948 began 12 years of small organ shop experience at the T. Eaton Company Organ Workroom. This little known venture built no particularly worthy instruments but provided the opportunity for Alan to work with over 40 personalities including many old-time craftsmen. When the workroom closed in 1960, he purchased the tools and goodwill from Eaton's and formed a service company. Casavant Frères appointed Alan Jackson to be their District Representative for Service in 1961 and for Sales in 1964. Of the 160 Casavant Organs built for the City of Toronto only a few have not been played, installed, repaired, rebuilt, voiced or tuned by Alan Jackson and Company. The company has serviced hundreds of pipe organs of all types from Sudbury, Ontario to the island of Bermuda.

Now an Honourary Life Member of the Royal Canadian College of Organists, Alan Jackson was chairman of the Toronto Centre of the RCCO from 1969 to 1971, a member of the National Council for 7 years, National Chairman of Publications in 1975 and was Chairman of the Toronto 1988 Convention of the American Institute of Organbuilders.

JAMES BAILEY, O.A.A., M.R.A.I.C.

A native of Edmonton, James Bailey has pursued a career which includes "practicing" both the organ and architecture, not only in that city, but also in Ottawa, Paris and since 1987, Toronto.

James is a graduate of the School of Architecture at Carleton University, Ottawa (1975) and has worked for a number of distinguished architectural firms including ARCOP Associates of Montreal and Douglas J. Cardinal Architect (Edmonton/Ottawa). During the 1980s he was the Design Coordinator for the Canadian Museum of Civilization.

He established his own architectural practice, James Bailey Architect, in 1992. The firm has a portfolio which includes churches, theatres, and other public buildings. In January of 2001 James was appointed Professor of Architecture at the School of Science and Technology at Sheridan College, Brampton, Ontario.

His training as an organist has been under William France, Dr. Godfrey Hewitt, André Fleury and William Wright. He has been a participant in organ academies and masterclasses in France under Michael Chapuis, Lionel Rogg, Raphaël Tambyeff and Fréderic Blanc. James has been the Director of Music and Organist of St. John's Church, West Toronto since 1995.

Index

152

153

154

Colophon

This book was set in 12/15 Cartier Book; chapter heads in 18/15 Cartier Book Bold; subheads in 12/15 Cartier Book Italic; captions in 10/12 Cartier Italics; and stop lists in 9/10 Cartier Book with Small Caps.

Cartier was designed as a book face by celebrated Canadian designer Carl Dair (1912-1967), and offered to the people of Canada as a Centennial gift in the year of his passing.

In 1997, Cartier was redesigned by Canadian type designer Rod McDonald. The beautifully crafted new version includes a full range of book faces, Regular, Medium, Bold, Italics, and Small Caps, as well as two Ornaments.

Without tampering with its original calligraphy-oriented design, Rod has transformed a problematic, never-finished typeface into a real contender as a book font. The use of it in this book honours the memory of Carl Dair, celebrates Rod McDonald's contribution to Canadian typographic excellence, and pays tribute to the craft of Canadian organ building.